McENROE

A RAGE FOR PERFECTION

A Biography by

RICHARD EVANS

Written in cooperation with John McEnroe

SIMON AND SCHUSTER

New York

Frontispiece: Sketch by Jamaican artist Virginia Burke.

Copyright © 1982 by Richard Evans
All rights reserved
including the right of reproduction
in whole or in part in any form
Published by Simon and Schuster
A Division of Gulf & Western Corporation
Simon & Schuster Building
Rockefeller Center
1230 Avenue of the Americas
New York, New York 10020
Originally published in Great Britain by Sidgwick & Jackson, Ltd.
SIMON AND SCHUSTER and colophon are trademarks of Simon & Schuster
Designed by Linda Dingler
Manufactured in the United States of America

10 9 8 7 6 5 4 3 2 1
Library of Congress Cataloging in Publication Data

Evans, Richard, date.
  McEnroe, a rage for perfection.

    1. McEnroe, John, 1959–   . 2. Tennis players
—United States—Biography.   I. McEnroe, John,
1959–   II. Title.
GV994.M33E9 1982   796.342′092′4 [B]   82-10474
ISBN 0-671-45932-5

CONTENTS

ACKNOWLEDGMENTS

One must, I suppose, qualify the term "biography" when the subject is a twenty-three-year-old athlete with much of his playing career still before him. A midterm report on a meteoric career would perhaps be a more realistic assessment of this attempt to chronicle the already considerable achievements of John McEnroe while, at the same time, presenting a side of the man that the public rarely, if ever, gets to see.

Given our itineraries, John McEnroe was elusive at times during the few short weeks we had at our disposal to collect material for this book. But that was not his fault. For a man who does not find it particularly easy or enjoyable to sit down and talk about himself, he was as generous with his time as I could have hoped. I expected no less because McEnroe, irrespective of his earlier public image, can be relied on totally to follow through on a commitment.

I must also thank his parents, John and Kay McEnroe, for their time and many kindnesses, especially John senior, who proved himself to be a painstaking copy reader, swooping down with a keen legal eye on everything from a misplaced comma to an error of fact. Suffice to say that any factual errors that remain are mine, as indeed are the opinions, some of which did not exactly gel with the McEnroe family's.

My thanks, too, to Dr. Robin Lester and his staff at Trinity School for their time and assistance, as well as John's many friends and acquaintances in the tennis world who answered my questions so patiently. A word of gratitude as well for my friends in St. Ann's Bay, Jamaica, who offered me a haven of tranquillity—not to mention a terrace with a breathtaking view—in which to get this whole project under way.

Finally a word of appreciation for my publishers on both sides of the Atlantic for proving that hard-cover books can be produced with speed and precision.

R.E.
New York, May 1982

PROLOGUE

What we have here is a hard man, born to achieve, destined to be misunderstood, unable to compromise, driven by an inner rage for perfection the ordinary man cannot comprehend. It is no use, therefore, asking of him the ordinary and the commonplace. For John Patrick McEnroe, Jr., is an original. There has never been a tennis player like him, and in a nomadic career that has brought me into contact with all manner of champions and achievers, I cannot think of anyone who encompasses his strange mix of qualities and faults. There are, of course, faults. This is not a eulogy. Not all of him is good, although much of the character is—often troublingly so. It is the personality that is flawed, particularly the one that appears in public.

It is the personality—that surly, pouting and often puerile personality—that obscures the character, that screens the substance of the man. And it is the superficial surface of that unfortunate personality that makes him anathema to so many, makes him, among certain sections of the sporting public, the least loved superstar of his era. But as he changes with time, so time will ultimately change the way he is perceived.

Had he been born with a shorter lower lip and a less furrowed brow, he would not have so much problem convincing people of his basic decency. Nor would every query and every quite rational question on court come across to his audience as a verbal assault from the original Angry Young Man. But John Osborne was before his time.

McEnroe, of course, is a reflection of the present age and, in an unkempt and slightly eccentric way, very much a representative of his generation. He is one of the most visible products of two decades of turmoil and questioning—a phenomenon, of course, that Osborne foresaw—which loosened the Establishment's grip on the convenient theory that elders were betters, and so fostered, especially in America, a generation that accepted authority, but only on merit. Even for the sons and daughters of the sober seventies, a positively benign bunch compared with the fanatical flower children who preceded them, a badge, a uniform and gray hair cannot command respect and obedience if the wearer is a fool. George Bernard Shaw, also ahead of his time, wrote in one of his plays, "It's all that the young can do for the old, to shock them and bring them up to date." In a certain sense, that is what McEnroe has been doing—like it or not.

Air Chief Marshal Sir Brian Burnett, chairman of the All England Club, has been quoted as saying that he thinks the biggest problem with McEnroe's behavior—referring, presumably, to his antics at Wimbledon in 1981—is that the new champion does not feel he has done anything wrong. That assessment is incorrect. McEnroe may disagree vehemently with the way the whole issue was handled but he is very well aware that, on certain occasions throughout his whole career, he has lost control of himself and has been very much in the wrong. But even his worst offenses, he feels, have been blown up out of all proportion. Why? Because he just doesn't think a tennis player shouting at an umpire should be treated with all the severity of a criminal offense in a world that is being savaged by criminals. He thinks the whole thing has got wildly out of hand. To his amazement and genuine disgust, he has seen his deeds lifted out of the sports section and emblazoned across the front pages and pontificating leader columns of newspapers all around the world. He finds that absurd and embarrassing because he doesn't regard himself as that important. And, of course, in a rational world, he would be right.

However, what McEnroe still does not quite comprehend, although he is getting there, is the deep offense he causes people—in America as well as in Britain and other more traditional nations—by the way his behavior is beginning to change the image of a sport known, even today, as "lawn tennis." The problem, of which McEnroe is only a reflection, lies in the vast and ever-widening gap between what people *think* the game is all about and what in fact it is. There is now an increasingly enormous difference between what the traditionalists wish for and what they get. As Rex Bellamy wrote in *The Times* following the infamous five-set battle between McEnroe and Jimmy Connors in the Benson & Hedges final at Wembley in November 1981, ". . . it also threw into total confusion all our pre-conceptions about the way professional sportsmen should conduct themselves before the paying public."

The problem lies not only in the intensity of the competitors, the enormous sums of money at stake, and the frequent incompetence of the officials, but inherently in the game itself. Partially because the old game of real or royal tennis, as practiced by Henry VIII and François I, was refined and streamlined by a middle-class major for the benefit of his genteel, Victorian, middle-class friends, tennis was camouflaged in an aura of totally deceptive gentility. Tennis is not a gentle game. Psychologically, it is vicious. That people are only just beginning to come to terms with this fact illustrates just how big a con trick has been perpetuated on the nonplaying tennis public—and even a few players, usually losing players—for decades.

"Anyone for tennis?" became an effete joke, used to depict a means of whiling away a lazy afternoon on a country house lawn. It is one of the game's glories that it may still be played that way if one is so inclined. But people conveniently forgot that it was one of Hollywood's great tough guys, Humphrey Bogart, who first uttered the phrase.

Played at the highest level of competitive skill, tennis is not unlike boxing stripped of violent bodily contact. Mentally it is even tougher and crueler than boxing or any other sport where the clock will do the winning for the participant. A boxer can build a lead on points over ten rounds and cover up for the remaining five until the final bell. A football team can run up an early score and rely upon its defense until the final whistle. A baseball team can score enough runs to be relatively safe from defeat.

But there is no such thing as a certainty or even a tie in tennis. It is a fight to the death; no prisoners are taken and time is irrelevant. A tennis player can lead 6–0, 6–0, 5–0, 40–love and still end up a loser if he lacks the nerve to go through with the dirty business of winning, if he does not possess the matador's courage to go in over the horns for the kill. Any top player will tell you that, in a tight match, he is more nervous when match-point up than match-point down. Why? Because he knows he is facing the ultimate test. If he fails, the chance may never come again.

Again like boxing, there is nowhere for a tennis player to hide, no chance while the ball is in play to take a breather, nor the respite for a batter of not coming to bat at all about two-thirds of the time when his team is at bat. There is no long walk between fairway and green. With tennis the spotlight is unceasing and unmerciful. Often for as long as four hours—something like two to three times the length of most athletic events—a tennis player must keep body and mind tuned to the highest pitch of concentration and competitive drive in a sport that demands control and precision as well as gut-wrenching bursts of speed and power. Anyone for tennis?

No . . . nor, surely, is it surprising that the sport breeds champions like John McEnroe. Volatile, mercurial, physically and technically disciplined to a degree that makes the average man look clumsy, and yet so emotionally wound up that an explosion of temperament can never be far from the surface—this is what tennis demands and this is what McEnroe has to offer. The two were made for each other.

"I tell you, to my mind, it's Borg who's abnormal," says McEnroe, who holds the icy Swede in high esteem. "I just don't know how he does it." Frankly, neither do I. Whatever the traditional tennis fan might wish for in his or her star performer, I find it far more natural, given what is required of them, that the game's greatest exponents behave like McEnroe, Connors and Nastase than Borg, Ashe or Vilas.

Having said that and having, I hope, highlighted the fact that tennis is not the game so many people perceive it to be, it must be said that McEnroe takes certain aspects of behavior to unacceptable extremes. Very rarely does it hurt his own game, for he has that ability which, to my knowledge, only Pancho Gonzales has shared, of being able to play in a rage. Within ten seconds of yelling at an umpire, McEnroe can hit a match-winning backhand of sweet precision. If he could not, he would have a far greater incentive to control himself. Like a child, he is often allowing his natural temper to run as far as the officials will let it. It is, after all, not his fault that he has never been thrown off court. On more than one occasion this blazingly honest young man has said to me, "Maybe I need to get defaulted. Maybe that would straighten my head out."

But the official tennis world, cowed by television, sponsors and the very real problem of depriving the paying public of a match, has never, at least prior to the stricter code of conduct introduced in 1982, had the courage to default McEnroe, even though he, Connors and Gerulaitis, to name but three, have all deserved it on rare but memorable occasions. Instead, some umpires pick on McEnroe like cowardly schoolboys who throw pebbles at someone and then run away. They warn him for hitting a ball harmlessly into the net, arrogantly stare him down when he makes a perfectly legitimate request, and nitpick at him for minor offenses that other players get away with day after day. But when he does explode, when he does go over the top in a fit of foul and boorish rage, the axe never falls. He is allowed to shout and scream and to continue the argument to an extent that is quite intolerable for the public and, more importantly perhaps, his opponent.

But let us not forget the reasons for these outbursts. McEnroe does not go on court looking for trouble. His objective, nutty as it may seem to us ordinary mortals, is to play the perfect tennis match: 6–0, 6–0, 6–0, no errors. Impossible? Of course, because tennis is too difficult a game for anyone to achieve that against a worthy opponent. But McEnroe sees no point in striving for anything less. So, as he is demanding so much of himself, he sees no reason why he should not demand as much of those around him.

"I don't regard it as unsporting or ill-mannered to tell a linesman he is doing a bad job, providing I don't swear at him," McEnroe has said in all innocence on numerous occasions. Before one questions his right to hold such an opinion, it has to be remembered that after a bad loss the first person calling his performance a disgrace is McEnroe himself. He never will be heard squealing when a critic raps him for his bad play. He has an extremely low tolerance for his own shortcomings on a tennis court—a fact that has always been vocally evident. McEnroe has been a screamer from way back. But, as we shall see in the chapters that follow, although he was a loud and rambunctious high school player, he was always screaming at himself. He never screamed at opponents and, because school matches were played without umpires, there was no one else to scream at. Certainly there was no one else to blame. If he lost, it was because he played badly and deserved to lose or, on occasion, because the other boy played better. Fair enough. McEnroe could accept that with surprisingly little remorse and no ill feeling.

But suddenly, on entering the big, cruel, adult world, young John discovered that unfair elements had been implanted all around him in the form of linesmen who took away points he had legitimately won. They didn't do it on purpose, of course. They simply made mistakes. But when McEnroe made a mistake he castigated himself. So why not castigate a linesman for a similar offense? Simplistic? Yes, to a certain extent, because McEnroe, a complex person in many ways, has nonetheless a very straight and simplistic view about right or wrong. If you are right you get rewarded; if you are wrong you get blamed. That was the way he was brought up by a strict mother and a father with a quick, hot temper who said what he thought with great vehemence and then got over it. What John didn't realize was that his own vehemence was just a bit too strong, too frightening even, for people to take.

But, of course, it wasn't just that. To explode on court, to find an outlet for all that compressed steam that builds up inside him, is a physical and emotional necessity. It is not only harmful but well nigh impossible for someone with an unusually high level of energy and tension burning away inside not to let it out—somehow. Ilie Nastase had a very similar problem, but being a natural clown, he managed to channel at least some of it toward genuine comedy and fun. McEnroe, although possessing a good sense of humor, is not a naturally funny man. And, in any case, he is much too serious about his tennis to risk trying to be funny in the middle of a match. So, inevitably, all that energy ignites a temper which, once aroused, is fueled by more and more of the same. Anyone who has lost his temper in a tense situation should be able to understand. It takes time to recognize and control the forces that swirl around inside us, and the task is made no easier when the self-examination has to take place in public all over the world, week after week. And McEnroe, remember, has been trying to do this in his early twenties.

It is not good enough, however, to protest that other players manage to control themselves, so why can't McEnroe? At the risk of being very obvious once again, the answer is simply that he is not like the others. In the accepted sense of the term, John McEnroe is not a normal individual. When the way that he plays tennis is considered, it would be amazing if he were. It is quite wrong to expect performers who have that touch of genius and whose special talent therefore stands out from the crowd to behave like everyone else. Look at Muhammad Ali, perhaps the most gifted heavyweight fighter of our time. Ali has about as much in common with McEnroe as Oscar Wilde had with James Joyce. With their personalities and problems they are poles apart, yet both share the experience of trying to come to terms with an exceptional talent. Neither has found conformity comfortable, yet McEnroe, the introvert like Joyce, will almost certainly learn to handle the spotlight and walk away before the flame consumes him.

It is difficult for parents to realize that they have a child who is fundamentally different from the others. His mother, Kay McEnroe, is only just coming to terms with the fact that John is just a little bit special. If one is too close to someone, it often takes a stranger to point this out. It was brought home to me very forcibly as far as McEnroe is concerned in November 1980 when John was heading for the Stockholm Open and, by chance, we both happened to catch the same Pan Am flight out of New York. He was in first class and I was in the Clipper section just behind, sitting in a row of three with a vacant seat between myself and a German lady who turned out to be Brigitte Barkley, an associate editor of *Geo* magazine. Somewhere over the Atlantic, McEnroe came back to chat and took the seat between us. Shy as ever with strangers, John spent most of the half hour talking to me and had very little to say to Ms. Barkley. But after he left us to go back and watch the movie, she turned to me and exclaimed, "That was amazing. I have never felt so much electricity and energy coming out of a human body before. Even when I wasn't talking to him or even looking at him, I was constantly aware of this special presence at my elbow."

But should he be treated differently just because he is special? If the question is posed in the form of "should he be treated more leniently within the laws of the game than anyone else?" then my answer is— most certainly not. He would never ask it nor expect it. Unfortunately the reverse is nearer to the truth. As the letters that have been pouring in to *Tennis World* and *Tennis Today* confirm, many spectators attending the final of the Benson & Hedges Championships at Wembley in November 1981 feel that McEnroe was victimized by the umpire, while Connors was allowed to get away with all kinds of infringements, often slyly disguised as humor. There is, of course, nothing sly about McEnroe. He comes at you head-on—forcing confrontation, demanding answers, increasingly unable to let an issue die a natural death.

"People recoil at that, especially in Britain where it has always been accepted in polite society that certain things are best left unsaid," points out Teddy Tinling, a master of etiquette. "He's a divisive force in our little world because he forces people to take positions they would rather not take."

It is partially for this reason that McEnroe has been treated so harshly in the press. The All England Club may be understandably unhappy at the way McEnroe escaped punishment for his outbursts at Wimbledon in 1981, but let no one suggest that he has not suffered other forms of punishment that are just as damaging as a monetary fine. Not all of us could withstand the psychological blow of seeing our names joined to a screaming headline, "Go Home, Superbrat," splashed all over the front page of a mass circulation tabloid just because we lost our temper. And it is not quite good enough to say that, as a highly paid public entertainer, McEnroe must put up with stuff like that. The punishment should fit the crime and, within the same sphere of reference, should be equally meted out.

Take, for example, Tony Shaw, an amateur sportsman, which in my view only makes his behavior worse. Who is Tony Shaw? Well might you ask. Just an Australian rugby captain who goes around setting such a fine example to the aspiring young players watching in the tens of thousands on television that he punches opponents in international matches. "As captain, the buck stops with him," wrote Barry Newcombe soberly in the London *Standard*. "The management ought to read the riot act to Shaw." Quite right, but even if the management followed Newcombe's excellent advice, nobody else bothered. Shaw continued to tour Britain, being offered all the deference and courtesy normally afforded a visiting captain, and no headlines telling him to get the hell back to Sydney. One could argue that it was a momentary lapse, I suppose. But Shaw *hit* someone. McEnroe never hit anybody in his life. Ah, but I know the answer. Shaw plays rugby, old boy. Physical sport, you know—man's game. Got to allow a little rough stuff once in a while. Got to give them a little chance to let off steam.

Am I one of the few to see a double standard operating here? If one accepts—as I certainly do—that a rugby player must be allowed to let off steam, which he has ample opportunity of doing at the bottom of scrimmage where no one can see, shouldn't a tennis player be allowed to shout now and again? After all, there is no scrimmage for him to hide in. Yet the tennis player, at least in McEnroe's case, is pilloried, abused and called a disgrace to his sport—that sweet, gentle, lily-white sport of lawn tennis. I don't find the situation either fair or reasonable.

I will accept without reservation that McEnroe, every bit as much—but not more than Shaw—deserves and needs to be disciplined even to the point in extreme cases of being ordered off. But let us keep it all in perspective if only because, as I hope the following pages will show, John McEnroe, while no saint, is more right than wrong, more good than bad. If the majority of the public are not yet convinced of that it is largely because of a problem that Octavius Caesar articulated so succinctly through Shakespeare's all-knowing pen in *Antony and Cleopatra:* "I do not much dislike the matter, but the manner of his speech."

True, but really, do manners maketh the man? Let us see.

1

A SWAMP PARTY
IN DOUGLASTON

By the early hours of New Year's Day 1982, the Swamp Party was facing a crisis. It was running out of beer. That was not altogether surprising, as over seventy young people were packed into the squat and far-from-beautiful house that stands at the bottom of Bayshore Drive, right on the very edge of Douglaston and Little Neck. Cars were backed up for several hundred yards along the steep curving road that leads past the large pond—soon to be iced over as the Big Freeze hit—and into the heart of the pretty and opulent dormitory community of Douglaston, New York.

The Swamp Party, so called becuase it was . . . well, kind of swampy as far as the well-heeled middle-class kids who attended it were concerned—hence its attraction—was definitely the place to be on this particular New Year's Eve. The house, made of overlapping slate and shingle, which give the less expensive buildings a scaly, reptilian appearance, was not really ready for the kind of invasion it received that night. It had been rented a few nights before by Tom Sobeck and John Dickey, a couple of local lads who were both carpenters by trade and were in the process of knocking the place into shape.

It was not, by consensus, the fault of the guest singer that part of the roof fell in. The three-piece band had been making quite enough noise on its own long before he had arrived, and the swaying press of bodies was sufficient to test the foundations of the whole building. But, in the absence of biblical trumpets to bring the walls crashing down, the place stood and the curly-haired young man at the microphone finally worked up enough confidence to get into a Stones song, "You Can't Always Get What you Want."

Maybe it was the irony of the title that caught someone's attention, for until then nobody had taken any particular note of exactly what was going on. Eventually somebody said, "Hey, do you realize who that is singing up there? That's John McEnroe and we're all behaving as if it's routine. It's weird, man." If I know John McEnroe at all, the man himself would have been very happy that everyone was taking it

as just routine. Much as he loves to sing and to envisage himself up there performing alongside Mick Jagger, he knows full well just how far he has to go with his musical ambitions before he can do anything more than make a token guest appearance at a charity concert.

So it was precisely because he knew nobody would give a damn that he was up there, wailing away into the mike at the Swamp Party on New Year's morning as his friends, most of whom had known him since they were all just out of diapers, searched around in desperation for the last cans of beer.

It is at parties in and around Douglaston and at local hangouts like Patrick's Pub, a bar as Irish as its name, and the Weeping Beech that McEnroe can shed the protective shell he carries with him around the world, and simply be himself.

It is a shame his public cannnot see Himself as Himself, to use an Irishism. Because Himself is not at all the kind of fellow you see projected through a television screen. So often his behavior invites his critics to see him as a loner, a man against the world, an aloof and cantankerous superstar with no more than a couple of close friends. Even on tour, where McEnroe does, indeed, have a few enemies, that loner image is something of a joke among the other players, who find him an agreeable and amusing locker-room companion.

Peter Fleming, who is probably his closest friend on or off the tour, played the joke for all it was worth during the Australian Indoors in Sydney last October. Fleming had agreed to do an interview for Australian television, and the cameras were set up in a small office right next to the locker room at the Hordern Pavilion. Although it was being taped, the set in the locker room was picking up the sound on closed circuit inside the stadium. Doug Mason of Channel 10 television opened up by asking Peter how he and McEnroe had come to play doubles together in the first place.

"Because neither of us had any other friends," Fleming replied with a wonderfully straight face. He might have been able to carry it through had not hoots of laughter erupted from Tom Gullikson, Peter Rennert and a few of the other players listening next door. At that Peter broke up, too, and the whole interview had to be started over.

The full absurdity of such a suggestion becomes readily apparent whenever McEnroe is playing in the New York area. Apart from really close friends like Doug Sabuto and Jimmy Malhame, various contemporaries are always dropping by the locker room. They could be childhood friends from Douglaston, old school chums or kids he used to play against on the junior circuit. I have often been impressed by the totally natural way he greets them. Neither he nor they ever seem embarrassed or even particularly conscious of the somewhat dramatic

Opposite: A soulful gaze from the new Wimbledon champion as he speaks at a rock concert in New York shortly after returning from England in 1981. "Ideally I'd like to be a rock star," says McEnroe, "but that's only a dream." *Linda Pentz*

change in status that has taken place in a remarkably short space of time. This, of course, can be partially explained by the fact that many of John's friends come from well-to-do families and are in the process of making successful starts to their own careers.

But even with fellow tennis players there is the same kind of easy "How've you been?" informality that completely precludes the awkward possibility of the conversation taking a stilted or one-sided tone. No struggling twenty-one-year-old player is going to walk up to a superstar, no matter how well he has known him in the past, if he thinks there is the remotest chance of being hit with a line like "I've just been making a couple of million bucks. What have you been doing?"

It says a lot for the way in which his contemporaries regard him that someone like Billy Porter can feel perfectly at ease going up to McEnroe at the Cove Racket Club on Long Island, as he did one day in December, to catch up with his news. Only four years before, McEnroe and Porter had been promising juniors around the eastern circuit. Now Porter was back home from a long European tour, having battled his way around the satellite circuit in France and Belgium in the hope of picking up a few precious ATP computer ranking points without which he would not even be able to qualify for the big Volvo Grand Prix events. Even though his results were improving a great deal toward the end, he would have been lucky to break even financially after four months away from home. McEnroe was at Cove that day to film a TV commercial for Dunlop—a company that is paying him in excess of half a million dollars a year over five years to use their rackets.

This discrepancy in their fortunes was not mentioned as the two of them chatted easily about their tennis and old times. There was no evidence of the shyness and suspicion with which McEnroe greets strangers and even acquaintances from the world at large. With friends of his own age, whom he got to know before fame and fortune swept him far from the comfortingly familiar boundaries of Douglaston, he is a totally different person. And even now, even with his duplex apartment in Manhattan and his condominium at Turnberry Isle in Florida, it is to Douglaston that he returns whenever he has some real time off from the circuit to recuperate and relax.

He spent the better part of three weeks there during the 1981 Christmas break. Apart from a couple of appearances for charity, he never touched a racket, which was good for him, and practically never exercised, which wasn't.

Most evenings would find him ensconced at a large round table at the Weeping Beech, a publike restaurant owned by an Englishwoman, Marta Brown, and her American husband, Russell. It is named after a tree that drapes itself with a forlorn kind of beauty over a little square situated just across the railroad tracks from the restaurant. Some typically callous developers wanted to chop it down a few years ago, but the good people of Douglaston raised a petition and forced the property men to leave their tree alone.

It was after that little triumph that the Weeping Beech was christened, and the place quickly became a favorite hangout for the neighborhood's younger set. Although quite spacious, the pub exudes a cozy conviviality which is enhanced by the brick walls behind the bar and the dark green decor around the dining area, where one can enjoy such exotic variations of traditional fare as a Weeping Bacon Cheeseburger. Arrayed along the walls are mounted heads of stags and other animals who fared less well than the tree. At one end of the bar there is a bison which bears a vague resemblance to the establishment's most famous client when he is passably content, and at the other hangs a bull moose wearing an expression many umpires would recognize as a fair imitation of McEnroe just after he has yelled at them.

McEnroe doesn't do much yelling at the Weeping Beech. Whatever his on-court behavior might suggest, he is not a hell-raiser in a bar. Certainly he is a babe in arms compared with the likes of Trevor Howard, Peter O'Toole and Richard Harris, who used to shake the branches of another pub with arborous connections, the Queen's Elm in London's Fulham Road, until the leaves fell off. But then all these esteemed members of the acting profession, most of whom are now under doctor's orders to give up the booze on pain of death, are hearty extroverts by nature. McEnroe, just as Irish as O'Toole and Harris in many other ways, is the precise opposite—a shy introvert who lets his music do his yelling for him when he is trying to relax.

Among friends he had grown up with, McEnroe was perfectly content to while away the evenings before Christmas at that large table by the door, getting quietly bombed on half a dozen beers as he bought round after round for people who joined the group for a while and then moved on.

This was his haven away from screaming crowds and probing press and fawning hangers-on, a quiet corner where he was known, respected and liked simply as a kid from down the road who made it big. Strangers would have no chance of penetrating that group because, like most good locals, everyone knows everyone at the Weeping Beech. And they all tend to get quite protective about their most famous son.

But generally he is treated just the way he likes to be treated at home—as one of the crowd. But, of course, the status he has achieved in the outside world offers his friends all the ammunition they need for a little gentle humor. Earlier in December, McEnroe had been named one of the twenty-five most intriguing personalities of 1981 by *People* magazine. The day after the Swamp Party, McEnroe was stretched out in the corner of another friend's house looking mildly incoherent after the exertions of the previous night, when a friend called Robbie Jackson gave him a playful nudge with his foot and demanded, "Hey Mac—say something intriguing!"

He didn't get a reply.

2

BEGINNINGS

Life did not begin for John Patrick McEnroe, Jr., in Douglaston, but in the U.S. Air Base Hospital at Wiesbaden, West Germany, at 10:30 P.M. on February 16, 1959, when Kay McEnroe was delivered—by an Austrian doctor—of an eight-pound son. The fact that this future Wimbledon champion was born in Germany was purely coincidental. He was born there because his father was serving in the U.S. Air Force, and he was taken home to America when he was nine months old. Needless to say, he remembers none of it—in fact, he remembers very little at all from his childhood—and Wiesbaden only became a reality for him when he went back there with his parents in 1980.

There was a nostalgic meeting with Frau Hanni Schultheis, in her eighties by then, who had been the landlady of the house in which John and Kay McEnroe had lived before moving into accommodations on the base. The McEnroes had been especially fond of Frau Schultheis, and they were delighted to see her looking so fit as she emerged from her house on Lahnstrasse to greet them. They were amused, too, to see her eyes open wide as she recognized the young man getting out of the car. "So this *is* your boy!" she exclaimed in amazement. "I have read about him, of course, and seen his pictures in the papers but I never connected the two. I thought there would be many McEnroes!"

But that is the closest attachment John has felt to Germany. "I suppose I had the choice of West German citizenship when I was twenty-one, but, of course, it never entered my head," he told me. "I haven't exactly been inundated with offers to play for Germany in the Davis Cup, either!"

So if it is unlikely that the Wiesbaden City Council will ever see fit to rename one of their streets McEnroestrasse, that is as it should be, for the youngster's roots were soon firmly planted in New York. Not, initially, in Douglaston, but prophetically enough in Flushing, where the young couple and their infant son took an apartment in one of those tall blocks that stand no more than five minutes drive from Louis

Armstrong Stadium, then a dilapidated open-air arena. Eighteen years later it was to be transformed into the National Tennis Center, just in time for a volcanic teenager to test the acoustics with a different pair of lungs, but as much flair and talent with his racket as old Satchmo ever blew down his horn.

By then, John senior had left the Air Force and was attending law school while Kay was busy giving birth to another son, Mark.* Although they made lifelong friends among some of the neighbors in Flushing, the McEnroes started looking for accommodations in a neighborhood more conducive to raising a family. An advertisement in *The New York Times* drew them to Douglaston, and although the apartment listed turned out to be no good, Kay was recommended to another nearby. So, in 1963, the McEnroes made a move that was destined to put the conservative little community on the map. There are, needless to say, some especially retiring residents of Douglaston who wished that had never happened.

By the time John was eight, the McEnroes had moved into a family-sized house in the exclusive Douglaston Manor district. It is a particularly pleasant neighborhood with the usual architectural variety that is common in expensive residential areas in America. No American with a little cash to spare wants his home to look like the one next door. Fronted by well-manicured lawns, many of the houses are wood-framed, while some are brick and others a combination that includes slate tiling.

Although far from rich, the McEnroes were beginning to feel financially comfortable by the end of the sixties. Despite the turmoil that was gripping so much of the nation, with race riots in Watts, Newark and Detroit fanning the flames of political unrest and a whole teenage generation seemingly at war with its parents, Douglaston remained something of a backwater, especially for families with children too young to be concerned with hippies in San Francisco or the draft call for Vietnam. The first time John's father ever set eyes on Douglaston he could not believe it was actually part of New York City. It is something of a municipal quirk that it should be so, for geographically it should really be designated as part of Long Island. But such technical details were of little importance to this young couple who were well on their way to fulfilling the American dream.

It is, I think, important to remember as we examine the McEnroe phenomenon that while John junior was a self-made multimillionaire

* The birth of their third son, Patrick, in 1966 provided John with one of his earliest memories—possibly because a friend beat him in the race back to the house to greet the arrival of baby brother from the hospital. By the time he was seven, John's competitive instincts were already at work.

24

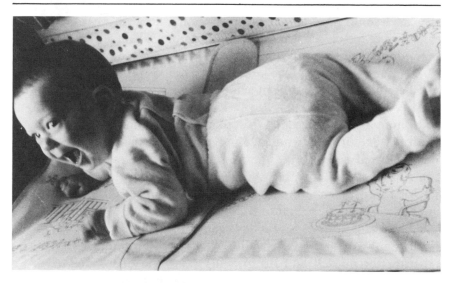

Above: The first scream? But, by the look of things, not too much to complain about at this stage. *Left:* John with brother Mark.

by the age of twenty-one, his father in a less spectacular but equally remarkable way had proved that hard work and intellect can in a very short time break down the class barriers that exist in American society. John junior's paternal grandparents were both born in Ireland. His grandfather, who finished his working life as a security guard at the Chase Manhattan Bank in New York, was born in Cavan and brought up in Dublin. His grandmother, a switchboard operator and clerk at a New York brokerage house, was born in County Westmeath. By the time their oldest grandson was nine, both had passed away.

Kay McEnroe, whose ancestry is half Irish and half English, feels that it is especially sad that Grandfather McEnroe did not live to see John soar to the top of the tennis world. "He was immensely proud of

John and could have had such fun boasting about his exploits to his cronies over a drink in one of his favorite pubs."

No doubt the old man would have been equally proud one day in 1974 when the McEnroe household waited breathlessly to hear whether John senior had been accepted as a partner in the prestigious New York law firm of Paul, Weiss, Rifkind, Wharton and Garrison. "I went shopping that afternoon, just so as to have something to do," Kay recalls. "I had dropped young John off for his tennis at Port Washington and I will never forget returning there to collect him and seeing him rush out to tell me, 'It's OK. Dad's just called. He's made it. He's in.' John was fifteen at the time and the only one of the boys to really comprehend what it meant to us."

It meant, of course, that a first-generation son of a working-class Irish immigrant had secured an extremely comfortable middle-class existence for himself and his growing family in one concerted leap. The American dream eludes the majority, but John McEnroe had turned it into reality several years before his own son began making the kind of money that transcends dreams.

For Kay, whose grandfather was born in Northumberland and came from a family of hatters, the upward journey through the echelons of American society had been only marginally less swift. Her own father had run a trucking company, and there were no immediate prospects of sumptuous middle-class living when she married an extrovert young New Yorker with a quick mind, a hot Irish temper and a sweet, almost cherubic smile. But she never had any doubts as to where they were heading. Kay McEnroe is a determined woman—charming, very feminine but also very strong.

"I always believed that, as a family, we would be successful," she told me. "I have never been one to accept second best. Mostly I was delighted with young Johnnie's work at school, but even if he got ninety-five percent in some test or other, I wanted to know what happened to the missing five percent. I think I probably pushed him harder than his father."

As I discovered while working with Allen Fox, a doctor of psychology and a former top-ten tennis player in the United States, scientific tests have proved that the classic formula for a successful son is a hard-driving mother and a father who is content to praise and encourage but not to dominate. In the book that Fox and I wrote, *If I'm the Better Player, Why Can't I Win?* we point out that in a study carried out by the psychologists Rosen and D'Andrade in 1959 there is a drastic difference with boys, in particular, between high achievers and low achievers depending on which parent does the pushing. There is nothing more intimidating for a young boy than to be driven by a father who keeps demanding, "Be like me!" A youngster of eight or nine, or even fifteen, can't be like his father—he is not as big, not as strong, not as experienced. If he is forced to compete on that unequal level, his ego is in grave danger of being crushed. The same is not true as far as the mother is concerned. The boy is not trying to emulate his mother. He is merely trying to please her.

Although John senior was a good basketball player, it was perhaps lucky that neither he nor Kay had played tennis before they joined the Douglaston Club—a social and sporting establishment that is housed in an imposing, white-painted, three-story building situated just a few blocks from the McEnroes' present house—the third they had occupied in Douglaston.

The Douglaston Club has five tennis courts, and it was not until their oldest son was ready to play that the McEnroes took up the game themselves. John's father was in his thirties by then so there was little danger of his turning into the kind of player who could continue to defeat a superbly gifted and highly coordinated young athlete. "I like to say that I beat John McEnroe for two straight years," says his father with an impish grin. "From the age of eight to ten!"

So, by virtue of his own extraordinary talent, John junior eliminated the possibility of his father becoming a threat in a sphere of endeavor that had immediately caught his interest. Instead of being a dominating, overwhelming figure, Dad was removed from the competitive arena in young John's life to that place where fathers are most effective—on the sidelines, cheering. The prodding and the pushing—when they were needed—came from Mother, who, one assumes, from the way she laughingly refers to herself as the Wicked Witch of the West, was the one who kept an iron hand on the household.

"Oh, John was disciplined; don't misunderstand me," his father emphasizes. "Just like all other children, he was sent to his room and he got beaten on the behind, sometimes with my hand, sometimes with a paddle. But not very hard. And I must admit that five minutes later I was often hit with remorse. I was depressed at the thought of having to hit my son."

Before all the armchair disciplinarians start nodding sagely and saying, "There you are! Told you that was the problem. Wasn't beaten hard enough or often enough," let me pose this question. Why should he have been? Because he deserved it? All the evidence points to the fact that he didn't. To a very large degree John McEnroe, Jr., could be described as a model child who was far too preoccupied with the considerable demands of being a success in the classroom as well as on the sports field to give his parents any real trouble.

That is not to say he wasn't high-spirited. It would have been difficult for a child with that amount of excess energy to be anything else. But apart from one run-in with the Port Washington Tennis Academy, of which more later, young John was never in serious trouble either at home or at school. "Even at the age of fifteen he wasn't allowed out during the week," says Kay, "but apart from one occasion, right at the end of his high school days when he turned up at three in the morning and got it in the ear, he was never late home when he went out on weekends. And I never, ever, had to tell him to go and do his homework in the evenings. He took responsibilities like that very seriously."

If this picture of a conscientious, self-disciplined child seems a little too good to be true considering the "spoiled-brat" image he earned— and, to some degree, deserved—by his behavior on court in later years, it must be emphasized that it is not purely the assessment of doting parents. Friends of his own age will confirm that, apart from sloppy dress and appalling table manners, John was certainly no worse than any of the other well-brought-up, middle-class kids of the neighborhood. More importantly, the headmaster of Trinity School will verify exactly the same.

The contradiction between McEnroe's public image and his private education—very private and very exclusive by American standards—is another intriguing and not altogether explicable facet of the story. If his behavior on court would lead one to think in terms of a teenager emerging from the vicious, undisciplined world of the blackboard jungle, it should be erased from the mind.

Below: Outside the McEnroe home in Douglaston just after John's seventh birthday in 1966. *Right:* Freckle-face, with a hint of things to come in the faraway expression in the eyes, just before his eighth birthday.

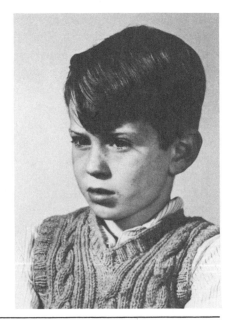

After attending Buckley Country Day School in Roslyn, not far from his home, John was sent at the age of thirteen to Trinity School on Manhattan's Upper West Side. Trinity is an old educational establishment not only by American standards but by English standards, too. It was founded in 1709 by royal charter of Queen Anne and is linked to a Dutch Reform School dating back to 1638. In 1894, Trinity moved to 139 West 91st Street from the parish church that had housed and sponsored it up till then. With the completion of the Hawley Wing in 1970, the school buildings, which include a modern twenty-story apartment tower, now occupy an entire city block. It is the oldest continuously operated school in New York City.

From the personality and appearance of the young headmaster, Dr. Robin Lester, with his tweed jacket, bow tie and pipe, to the atmosphere that pervades the imposing entrance hall and clasrooms, Trinity exudes an air that is instantly recognizable to anyone with an Establishment education. It is a coeducational day school with over eight hundred pupils—its size being partially dictated by the fact that it serves as both preparatory and high school, taking some children from kindergarten age right through to the time they leave for university at eighteen. The academic standard is high—a fact borne out by the number of leading universities that accepted Trinity students from the class of '81 alone—ten went to Yale, nine to Cornell, seven to Vassar, and four each to Harvard and Princeton, among numerous others.

Trinity, in other words, is accustomed to handling the cream of the crop, as far as Manhattan families are concerned; and on his arrival in 1972, there was nothing to suggest that a certain Master McEnroe, one of the relatively few children who had to travel in from the suburbs, would end up being one of the school's most famous sons or, indeed, one of its biggest benefactors.

"If you had lined up all 300 boys in his approximate age group when he arrived here and asked us to place them in the order of who was most likely to succeed as an international athlete, John would have come in 299," Dr. Lester told me. "He had a cherubic, full-moon Irish face, an unimpressive torso and was outright pudgy with dimples on his knees. However it didn't take us long to realize he had amazing hand-eye coordination."

Dr. Lester was the history master in McEnroe's time at Trinity, later becoming headmaster. He remembers John as a slightly above-average student in an average year, a shy boy with scrawly handwriting who always sat at the back of the class.

"But being shy didn't mean he was silent," Dr. Lester laughed. "He had a healthy skepticism about certain historical figures and was not afraid of voicing his opinions. He was what I would call a master of the back-of-the-room witty aside. One could say the back row found him pretty entertaining. But with me he never crossed that line which would have made him a smart ass or a troublemaker."

Although math was his best subject, John McEnroe was a good Latinist in a school that prides itself on what is described as "the current healthy state of classics at Trinity." That alone would make Trinity a happy rarity among American high schools, but much of the credit for this must go to the English-born classics master, Frank Smith. Now nearing the age of retirement, Smith was apparently the master who understood McEnroe best and who struck up the easiest rapport with a youngster who always had a problem opening up to adults. Again McEnroe's contradictory nature rears its complicated head. A middle-aged Englishman teaching classics would hardly seem to be the most likely candidate to secure McEnroe's trust.

By the time he was fifteen, John was considered mature enough to travel to school each day by himself. The journey was a daunting one and the fact that his parents were comparatively at ease with the idea of allowing him to make it five times a week illustrates as well as anything the confidence they placed in their son's common sense and instinct for survival. Undoubtedly those daily journeys gave McEnroe a new and not very savory look at the world and taught him how to stand up for himself. New York City is not a place where manners count for very much. It is a jungle at the best of times—a concrete jungle inhabited by every species of humanity, including some who make wild animals seem positively benign. Quite a few of the less desirable ones lurk in the vicinity of Penn Station, and it was there that young John McEnroe, still quite small for his age, had to change trains every day. The journey from Douglaston to Penn Station takes thirty minutes, and from there John had a four-minute walk to the subway in order to catch the 7th Avenue IRT line up to 91st Street—another twenty minutes away. It was a long haul.

"I wouldn't say I liked the idea very much," Kay admits. "But there wasn't really an alternative solution, so I just tried not to dwell on the possibilities. And John was very good about getting home on time."

As it was, young John was only mugged once. The guy hit him a glancing blow in the face, and the victim reacted in the best way possible for someone with a very fast pair of legs. He ran. Another incident McEnroe remembers from all those subway rides, rubbing shoulders with the smart office workers and the drunks and riffraff of that bewildering city, is absolutely typical because it spotlights so accurately the kinds of things that attract his attention, the things that he finds important in life: "A man with a sign around his neck saying 'Deaf & Dumb' was shuffling past us on the train and someone called his bluff and goes, 'You're not deaf, you asshole' or something really bad like that, and just for a split second, I saw the guy react. He had his back to us as the man said it so, of course, I knew he had heard. That taught me a lot about New York City and what kind of phoniness there is around."

Already McEnroe was deciding one of the things he liked least in the world was a phony. Nor did he have much tolerance for cheats. Dr. Lester, who as a tennis fan was accustomed to attending Wimbledon each year long before a kid called McEnroe walked into his history class, used to watch John play many of his school matches and he remembers one when the other boy was obviously cheating on line calls.

"Of course, there were no umpires or linesmen, so everyone was on his honor as far as line calling was concerned," Dr. Lester pointed out. "But things were getting so bad in this particular match that eventually John walked up to the net and asked the boy if he was really sure of that last call. He was giving him a final opportunity but the fellow missed his cue. So John simply went back and proceeded to cut him to ribbons. He just humiliated him with his tennis."

This is interesting, not just because of McEnroe's reaction to a cheat, but because throughout his junior years it seems that he was often playing within himself. The full force of the intensity that we see from him now virtually every time he walks on court was missing in those days, except when he was playing against opponents of near equal ability in national junior tournaments. The primary reason for this would seem to be that tennis was by no means the sole recipient of his interest and energy. Apart from his academic work, he played numerous sports, including basketball, baseball, soccer and football and excelled at them all. But another reason seems to stem from a reluctance to make his opponents look complete fools—unless they gave him good reason to.

Soccer was a game that matched his fast-moving temperament and made satisfying demands on his abundance of skill. It was also, after tennis, the sport he played with the greatest success at Trinity. He played left wing and was the school's leading goal scorer in his senior year when Trinity led the Ivy Preparatory Leagues. Utilizing what soccer writers might describe as a cultured left foot, he perfected the curving cross and was even known to score directly from corner kicks.

But despite McEnroe's love of games and the amount of time it took him to pursue them, Dr. Lester insists that it never affected his work. Nor did he ever ask for any time away from school to play tennis. "Neither John nor his parents asked for any special favors on that score," says the headmaster. "Even in his final year when he was rushing off on a Friday afternoon to catch a plane to play in some pro tournament or other—I remember one weekend he had to play Nas-

Above: Judging by the style displayed here, and his goal-scoring record for Trinity School, John McEnroe could have developed into the home-grown soccer star that America is searching for, had not tennis intervened. *Trinity School Left:* McEnroe signs posters for young fans from his old school, Trinity, at a fund-raising event during the Tournament of Champions at Forest Hills. *Lois K. Gerard*

tase and Lutz—he was always back in class on Monday morning well prepared, obviously having found time to do his homework. And it wasn't easy work either. He was doing advanced placement calculus, which is basically a very difficult program."

The only event in his school career that John did miss was an important one—his graduation ceremony. "He was very upset about it, but that was one occasion when tennis did come first—with our blessing," explains Dr. Lester. "We made playing in the French Open and Wimbledon his Senior Year Project. So he was absent when all his classmates—a very bright and well-adjusted group of young people like Alex Seaver and Tony Kiam, who are now both at Harvard, and Laura Hughes, who is already a successful young actress on Broadway—graduated at the traditional ceremony which is held at Trinity Church near Wall Street. I know John would have loved to be there."

But quite apart from the fact that both brothers followed him to Trinity—Patrick is still there and is, according to his headmaster, one of the best students of the current crop—John did not turn his back on his old school. On May 5, 1981, the Tuesday evening of the WCT Tournament of Champions at Forest Hills, Trinity hosted a dinner on the club grounds to raise money for the McEnroe Scholarship Fund. "The aim of this fund," John explained to his guests, "is to help provide a first-rate education to some New York City children who might otherwise be unable to afford it."

The only thing that went wrong that night was that McEnroe lost, somewhat unexpectedly, to Brazil's Carlos Kirmayr in the first round. That, however, did not stop him appearing to sign autographs and answer questions posed by Trinity students and their families. According to the Trinity newsletter, McEnroe deserved thanks, not simply for raising $14,000, but for providing a fine example for everyone through his generosity and grace under pressure.

He certainly does set us a wonderful example in that respect [says Dr. Lester]. He is especially good with the parents, somewhat surprisingly advising them to keep things in perspective and allow their children to enjoy all the sports and facilities available to them and to resist the temptation to specialize too early.

But, of course, one can't ignore the criticism he has quite rightly received for some of his behavior on court. That is very disappointing to us but I don't have any answers. An Irish temper obviously runs through the family. Mark had a few problems with that in basketball games, but John was never out of control when he played sport here at Trinity. Noisy, certainly, but he was always complaining about himself, not others. I just hope he will learn to live more comfortably with the mantle of the No. 1 player in the world around his shoulders.

3

JUNIOR TENNIS

If John McEnroe, the unruly superstar, was an exemplary student and loving son, who gave teachers and parents a great deal less cause for concern than many youngsters of his generation, the surprises and contradictions that litter his early teenage years do not end there. For, as a junior tennis player, this wonderfully gifted athlete, who was to burst into the public consciousness as a Wimbledon semifinalist at the age of eighteen, was never ranked No. 1 in the United States at any age, although he did attain No. 1 in the junior rankings of the great big world he was to dominate so soon.

Considering the natural ability that was evident from the moment he first kicked, hit or threw a ball as a tiny child and the hunger for victory that was lurking in his makeup throughout his childhood years, I find this to be one of the greatest anomalies in a life story that is filled with a bewildering array of unlikely and often illogical data.

However, Tony Palafox, the patient, good-natured former Mexican Davis Cup player who, along with the great Australian coach Harry Hopman, has been responsible for McEnroe's technical development, had coincidentally borne witness to an equally sudden flowering of talent in his own career. Ironically, it concerned another left-handed Hopman protégé: a shy, freckle-faced Australian who was to become McEnroe's idol—Rod Laver.

"I used to practice all the time with Rod in 1958," Palafox recalled. "There was plenty of opportunity to do so that year because Rod was losing in the first or second round almost every week. I remember we finished the tour in Budapest and I said, 'See you next year.' But there was a lot less time to practice the next year because Rod was in all three Wimbledon finals—singles, doubles and mixed!

"I saw a similar sort of change come over John. There comes a moment when the head connects with the body. Everything clicks into place and the improvement is very fast. I must admit I never thought

John would become so good so quickly. When he was sixteen he was only one of five guys I was looking after—Rennert, Fromm, Friedman and Kohlberg were the others—and although John had the greatest natural ability, there really wasn't much to choose between them."

Palafox was working as a coach at the Port Washington Tennis Academy on Long Island in 1970 when Kay McEnroe arrived one afternoon with her eleven-year-old son. Tony didn't need more than a few minutes on court with the child to recognize the easy, fluent talent he possessed with a racket, and he had virtually made up his mind to accept him into the Academy by the time he received a phone call the following day from Chuck McKinley, the 1963 Wimbledon Champion. Apparently McKinley, now a Wall Street businessman, was calling at the request of someone he knew who was acquainted with John McEnroe, Sr.

"What do you think of that kid McEnroe who came to see you yesterday, Tony?" Chuck asked.

"He's OK," Palafox replied. "He's got a good feel and can hit shots from all parts of the court. I reckon he's worth a try."

Within twenty-four hours, forms for enrollment in the Port Washington Academy arrived, signed by his father, and young John was all set for several hours of serious tennis instruction each week.

In September that year, at about the same time that Ken Rosewall, one of his earliest protégés, was winning the U.S. Open a few miles away at Forest Hills, Harry Hopman saw McEnroe for the first time. "It was a Friday evening when some of the more talented kids were there and John made an immediate impression on me," Hop told me from the camp he now runs in Largo, Florida, having left the Academy in 1975. "Although his serve is nothing like the one he has now, he reminded me a bit of Neale Fraser [another of Hop's Wimbledon Champions] because, apart from also being a leftie, he was always trying to do different things with the delivery."

Now Frank Sedgman, Lew Hoad and Rod Laver are names Hopman mentions in the same breath as the young man he helped to guide to that place in the tennis atmosphere that, at various moments over the past three decades, has seemed to be reserved exclusively for pupils of the Hopman school—No. 1 in the world.

Quite apart from the fact that he is not Australian, there are some other rather obvious differences between McEnroe and other stars from Hop's stable. During his days as the most successful Davis Cup captain in history, the tough little Aussie built his reputation on discipline, and consequently a great deal of tennis talent belonging to the likes of Bob Hewitt, Ken Fletcher and Marty Mulligan fled Australia in the sixties because it could not tolerate the Hopman regime. So how, in turn, can Hopman tolerate McEnroe? Has this legendary figure, still sprightly and alert after a serious hip operation in his seventy-fifth year, mellowed?

Hop had just come off court after a few more hours coaching in the burning Florida sun when I phoned, and the suggestion was met with a laugh as dry as tinder from the Australian bush. "I like John's temperament," he replied flatly. "He is always striving so hard for the perfect shot. I like players who get angry when they fail to meet the standards they set themselves. John Bromwich was like that. I remember him throwing up his hands at the White City in Sydney as if he was praying for help."

"Despite his generally quiet demeanor, wasn't Rosewall that way?" I suggested. "So often I've seen him throw down his racket in disgust after missing a backhand."

"Kenny just didn't like to lose a point," Hop replied with a quick, revealing insight implying, surprisingly perhaps, that McEnroe is more interested in perfection for its own sake than the victory which perfection inevitably will bring.

As far as tennis is concerned, there may be some truth to that, for the dream of playing the perfect tennis match is never far from McEnroe's mind. But there is no denying the strength of the competitive drive, the need, when the mood takes him, to win just for the sake of it, for the thrill of a challenge. Kay McEnroe remembers being at the Douglaston Club one afternoon when John was still a youngster and there was a medal offered for the child who could swim one hundred laps of the club pool. This was more an endurance test than anything else, and Kay didn't expect the idea to interest her son very much, because swimming had never been a sport at which he had excelled to the same degree as tennis or football. However, when she was about to return to the house, John hung back and mumbled, "I'll see you later. I think I'll give the swimming competition a try." Later on in the afternoon, Kay returned and John was standing there with the medal. "Yes, I won it," he shrugged. "No big deal."

What drove him then? The idea of doing something, just about anything, better than a bunch of his peers obviously was sufficient to overcome the laziness that is also a distinct yet, once again, contradictory part of his makeup. Here we have a child who is always quite voluntarily on the go, bursting with energy and drive; a child who rushes into the house at lunchtime during the school holidays and grabs whatever his mother is cooking and rushes out again; a child who never has the patience to read a book other than for schoolwork because he's always involved in a game of soccer or softball or ice hockey on the frozen pond down the road. And this child is lazy?

The Douglaston Club under snow. It was on the clay courts at the back of this imposing building that young John hit his first tennis ball in the summer months. *Mary Carillo*

Tony Palafox seated in front of a thoughtful John McEnroe, Sr. *K. M. Finnerey*

"When Hop came to the Academy, John used to try and hide," says Palafox. "Hop believed in drills and lots of hard work, and John didn't like hard work. He never wanted to practice as much as the other guys."

A truant from tennis practice but a self-disciplined stickler for homework? However unusual that might be, there can be no faulting McEnroe on his priorities. School was serious, tennis was fun. School was difficult while tennis, for McEnroe, was easy. So why turn fun into drudgery? According to the logic that was forming in this boy's astute young mind, one should only be serious about the things one needs to be serious about. Work fell into that category because his parents were constantly reminding him of the need for a good education. But tennis practice certainly didn't. Tennis was time off, time in which to relax. If one wants to know why McEnroe takes his matches in such deadly earnest, the clue is here. Matches have replaced work while practice in his mind is still time off. In this respect he is the complete opposite of Laver, who spent more hours on the practice court than any player I've ever known, save perhaps Brian Gottfried.

Here, I think, we get another inkling of another wholly unlikely aspect of the McEnroe character. Then and now John McEnroe is at heart the true amateur sportsman. I realize how preposterous that may sound to anyone who has only observed the millionaire athlete screaming his head off at some underpaid linesman. But that is McEnroe all wound up in the competitive arena. In a sense he becomes a different human being the moment he walks on court to play a match. But there is an equally real side of him that, in an earlier calmer age, would have fitted perfectly into the world of amateur sport as it was once played—and still is played, for that matter, in less commercial atmospheres on a weekend afternoon. One can just see him wandering around a tennis club with his socks around his ankles, clad in the same pair of wrinkled shorts that he had worn to whip some bemused opponent the week before, the arms of his school sweater wound around his neck. Once on court the same intensity would have been evident. But generally, both on court and off, I suspect that McEnroe would have been much happier amidst the camaraderie of the amateur sporting world with its code of honor than the code of conduct he faces on today's cutthroat professional circuit.

The code of honor that existed in American junior tennis, as far as players calling their own lines was concerned, suited young McEnroe just fine—even if a fear of cheating his opponent out of points occasionally worked against him. The rule in the junior ranks was that a linesman could be called for if either player felt there was a problem. According to his father, John never called for a linesman while competing in junior tournaments, and in fact Mr. McEnroe was rather startled one day at Port Washington when Herman Newfield, who was helping to run junior programs at the Academy, came up to him and said, "You know, you should never let John go on court without a linesman."

"For a moment I was taken aback," John senior recalls. "I thought 'What is he saying?' But then Herman went on to explain that he had never seen a youngster call so many close balls against himself as John. He said he was just cheating himself out of points by trying to be too fair and that it would be better for him to have a linesman."

Knowing John as I do, I have no difficulty believing that story, despite its rich irony. Even if the paranoia and virtual persecution complex that he suffers from today are beginning to affect his judgment—and there is no doubt that he is starting to complain needlessly about perfectly good calls—McEnroe's outbursts on court are almost always triggered by one of two things: his own imperfect play or what he considers to be an injustice. The inability—or the blind, stubborn refusal—to accept that life is a journey through a minefield of injustices lies at the source of many of McEnroe's problems, and his hatred of anything less than direct or honest would make it perfectly plausible for him to steer well clear of giving an opponent even the slightest opportunity of calling him a cheat. In his naive and unsullied youth, I am sure John would have happily given away a few points rather than leave himself open to charges like that.

So the "amateur" code would have suited McEnroe very well in many ways, and his affinity with that old-fashioned amateur world—an affinity that is well camouflaged, obviously, by all that intensity and less than gentlemanly behavior—struck me most forcibly when I saw that marvelous film *Chariots of Fire*. I realized then that Harold Abrahams, back in the twenties when professionalism was considered a nasty and probably contagious disease, was far more professional at heart than McEnroe is today in this age of multimillion-dollar paychecks. Just as Borg has his Bergelin and Vilas his Tiriac, so Abrahams, contrary to all Olympic ethics, became a pioneer of the whole coaching concept by having his Sam Mussabeni, the small Italian, played so movingly in the film by Ian Holm, who dared not watch his pupil race, not even from the back of the crowd. McEnroe has no Mussabeni. Only in recent months, when a friend such as George Martin, a New York restaurant owner, sometimes acts as a kind of part-time assistant at tournaments to provide a buffer between John and all the people who want bits of his time, does he even have someone with him. But it certainly isn't a coach. On the very rare occasions that Palafox watches one of his matches, the advice is kept to a minimum. For a top professional, McEnroe's prematch preparation is just a trifle cavalier. As we have noted already, serious practice is a sort of last resort, used only if he hasn't been playing enough matches. Stroke production problems tend to get worked out in the doubles, which McEnroe, quite apart from enjoying them, uses in lieu of practice.

But even in doubles one sees priorities being adhered to that have little to do with the cold competitive realities of the circuit where expert doubles players will frequently team up solely in the hope of earning money and points, even though they may have barely spoken a civil word to each other before. Such opportunism is perfectly legitimate and realistically professional. But it doesn't interest McEnroe. He will only play with friends. If Peter Fleming is not available, he will ask Ferdi Taygan, Peter Rennert or Bill Maze to be his partner. And if there is no one at a particular tournament whom he considers a genuine friend, he won't play doubles at all that week. Again it is an attitude that smacks more of the amateur than the professional.

So there were no real problems with opponents or officials in the junior ranks, although, as his father readily admits, John quickly gained a reputation for being a very intense competitor—and a very noisy one, too. But all the "hootin' and hollerin'," as Mr. McEnroe describes it, was self-directed anger at his own poor play.

Apart from Hopman and Palafox, there were a few other people, some speaking from experience and some from instinct, who realized that this sloppy, pudgy kid was destined to become something special. One of them was Gene Scott, publisher of *Tennis Week* and a Forest Hills semifinalist in 1967. Having guided Vitas Gerulaitis through his formative years, Scott is always quick to spot exceptional young players on the eastern seaboard, and he played doubles with McEnroe in a local tournament when John was only fifteen. "I knew immediately he was going to be a class player," says Scott. "He produced angles I had never even thought of. Anyone who has an instinctive grasp of how to play doubles at that age should have no trouble in reaching the top."

But no one, perhaps, has an earlier memory of McEnroe on a tennis court than Mary Carillo, whose family still lives just a few blocks away, toward the wide expanse of water called Little Neck Bay. A year older than John and a fine athlete herself, Mary used to join in all the boys' games that were played on the nearby sports field. Given Mary's happy, outgoing disposition—all that sunny Italian charm melting the Irish mist—I have no doubt that she helped John overcome any initial shyness he might have had with older children, as well as helping him develop his natural athletic talents.

"We played everything—basketball, football, ice hockey," Mary recalls. "John was by far the best athlete around. His was the team you definitely felt like being on! But we also used to play a lot of tennis against each other when he was eleven and twelve. There was no problem getting courts at the club, and we used to play five sets regularly during the summer months."

Eventually John suggested to Mary that she too take lessons at Port Washington, and even there they occasionally got to play. "But that was as a result of disciplinary action taken by Harry Hopman," Mary pointed out. "Hop used to get mad because John would start dinking around and using all this loose-wristed stuff to produce outrageous spins in the middle of some straightforward drill. So Hop told him that if he wanted to play like a girl he could come over to our court and play the real girls! John didn't think much of that, and it was a pretty long face that used to join us. But he got over it pretty quick."

It was back at the Douglaston Club, however, that Miss Carillo turned prophet and caught sight of a very accurate reflection in her crystal ball. "It must have been when he was about thirteen," Mary said. "He was beating up on me pretty bad by then. But at home I was still one of the best players around, so he was quite happy to play with me.

"One day after we had just finished another heated battle I sort of collapsed courtside, and just as a kind of reaction from having to deal with all that talent, I suppose, I said, 'Oh, God, John, you're going to be the best player in the world.' "

Typically, McEnroe wasn't impressed.

"Oh, shut up," he replied, using a little mild aggression to hide a combination of embarrassment at the compliment and of realization, even then, of the enormity of what Mary had just suggested. "You haven't seen anyone play. You can't judge."

There is no doubt that McEnroe already realized that he had talent but, like any schoolboy, he was in awe of the great champions of the time. When Mary mentioned the best player in the world, John had only one frame of reference in his own mind—Rod Laver, his idol. Mary didn't know as much about Laver as John did, but she knew something exceptional was developing in Douglaston, and it just seemed to her that anyone of that age who could play so many different strokes so easily simply had to end up being the best player in the world. She was right.

There was early evidence that she would be proved correct, in Paris in 1977, when she and John were both competing at the French Open for the first time. "We looked at the sign-up board for the mixed doubles and said, 'Why not?' " It is not hard to imagine the thrill they both felt when they went on to win the title. "Mixed doubles champions at the French Open! Wow, we could hardly believe it. Four of our friends from Douglaston just happened to be in Europe, and we all sat around the table and popped the champagne and made jokes about how half the town had come to Paris to see us win the mixed. It was a great evening!"

But that is jumping ahead of the story. Paris and champagne were still a little way off when the one serious blemish on McEnroe's career in junior tennis occurred. Sadly enough, it involved the Port Washington Tennis Academy, an institution that had been so good for him at the very start of his career. The Academy, which continues to thrive today under the directorship of Alex Aitchison, an Australian friend of Hopman's, is the brainchild of its owner, Hy Zausner, a rich American with a genuine philanthropic bent. The facilities at the Academy are such that the place runs at a loss, despite being filled to capacity with about a thousand students attending classes at junior and senior levels at various times each week and a thousand more playing in one of the 150 tournaments held there each year. It survives only through tax exemption as a nonprofit organization and generous financial contributions from Zausner himself.

A happy couple from Douglaston celebrate in the Parisian spring—Mary Carillo and John McEnroe after winning the French Open mixed doubles title in 1977. *Le-Roye Productions*

Unfortunately Zausner appears to have been a little high-handed in the way he dealt with an incident that occurred, not at the Academy itself, but during a junior tournament held at the Concord Hotel in upstate New York in 1976.

"It was a schoolboy prank that got out of hand," admits McEnroe. "One night Peter Rennert and I decided we would create a little havoc in the girls' dorm. So Peter got a fire bucket and positioned himself outside the door while I lit a small towel we had rolled up and threw it into the room."

Apparently Rennert then leaped into the room as McEnroe yelled "Fire!" and sprayed the place with water, being careful to hit the burning towel and not being too careful about what else he hit—beds, clothes, girls in nightdresses, girls half-undressed—pandemonium, hysteria, great fun.

"Except, of course, that it was damned dangerous and therefore an irresponsible thing to do," says McEnroe, looking back with the wisdom of the passing years.

The story got back to Zausner because one of three boys—and McEnroe is still not sure which—ratted on Peter and himself. The result was a letter that turned up at the McEnroes' house in Douglaston a few days later, addressed to John Jr., informing him that he had been suspended from the Academy, along with Rennert, for the rest of the summer.

"I thought it was a shocking way to handle the situation for two reasons," John's father told me. "Firstly, Hy Zausner knew me quite well enough to pick up the phone and, at the very least, warn me that the letter was coming. That would have been basic courtesy, especially as John was one of his best students and we, as a family, were pretty enthusiastic supporters of the place, having sent Mark and Patrick, our two younger boys, there as well.

"Secondly, I didn't quite understand what it had to do with the Academy. The incident hadn't occurred at Port Washington, and John and Peter were not playing at the Concord as representatives of the Academy. Without condoning in any way what had occurred, I was frankly shocked and disappointed at Zausner's action."

Although it was made clear to John that he would be welcome back for the winter semester, the feeling in the McEnroe household, always a proud and tight-knit family group in times of crisis, was that it would be better for the star pupil to continue his tennis education elsewhere.

"We put no pressure at all on the other boys, but Mark immediately said that he had no wish to go back to a place where his brother was not welcome," said Mr. McEnroe. "I felt like hugging him for that kind of loyalty."

Peter Rennert, Stanford teammate and one of McEnroe's
closest friends, is now a sharp-
witted member of the pro
tour. *Richard Evans*

The decision was certainly made easier by the fact that both Hopman and Palafox had left Port Washington by that time, and Tony was
working at Cove Racket Club, which was situated even nearer to
Douglaston than the Academy. So, fortuitously as it turned out,
McEnroe and Palafox were reunited.

"I hadn't seen him for seven or eight months when he came to work
with me at Cove, and he had obviously improved," Palafox recalls.
"But he needed some work on the backhand, and to start with we spent
at least fifty percent of the time working on a topspin backhand. Until
the age of sixteen he could only hit the shot flat or with underslice."

Thus, in the quieter and more personally concentrated atmosphere
of a small club, working with a man he trusted implicitly, McEnroe
was able to add the finishing touches to a game that was to blossom so
suddenly a year later.

Rennert, meanwhile, had moved with his family to California, so he,
too, never returned to Port Washington, although it was thought at the
time that both he and his parents accepted the disciplinary action as
just. In a *Tennis Week* interview with Linda Pentz in December 1981,
Alex Aitchison was quoted as saying that Rennert admitted the Academy had been right. That remark prompted Rennert to write the following letter to *Tennis Week,* which was published in the January 30
issue of 1982:

Just to set the record straight, I would like to correct a quotation attributed
to me by Alex Aitchison. . . . In their suspension of John McEnroe and my-

self in 1976, not only did I not think they were right, but I thought they acted hastily and insensitively without even attempting to hear our side of the story. . . . I talked with Hy Zausner afterwards in an attempt to understand their point of view and apparently Alex chose to interpret my comments then as an acknowledgement that "they were right." . . . I didn't think so then and now that I have graduated from the junior ranks and have, I hope, attained a more mature point of view, I still don't think so.

Even before he left Port Washington, McEnroe had decided that all the other sports he enjoyed and excelled at would have to take second place to tennis or be eliminated altogether. Football was one of the first to go. Being the best athlete on the team and the one with the quickest brain, McEnroe had inevitably ended up as quarterback. But at fourteen McEnroe was still small for his age and therefore in ever-increasing danger of being seriously mauled by some opposing giant. His parents had been trying to persuade him to give up the game for fear that he would suffer an injury that would wreck his chances of realizing his full potential in tennis. But it was Horace Reid, a big black kid at the Academy who played on the pro circuit for a few years later on, who finally got John to listen to reason. "You're crazy playing football, man," Reid told him. "Especially as a quarterback where you're throwing with your left arm. That's your tennis arm you are putting at risk. Don't do it." Thanks to Horace that was the end of John McEnroe, quarterback.

By the time he was fifteen, McEnroe was becoming a veteran of the junior tournament circuit. His parents had taken turns escorting him to events in the East and Midwest during the early years, but increasingly John, despite his shyness with adults, was happy to travel on his own, finding no difficulty in enjoying his time at tournaments with kids his own age.

Eliot Teltscher, the wiry little Californian who was to dog Mc-Enroe's footsteps all the way into the world's top ten, remembers playing him for the first time in Dallas when they were both fourteen. "I know we had an umpire for that match, which was kind of unusual, because it was Anne Smith's father [Anne is now a top player on the women's tour], but mostly we were calling our own lines," Teltscher recalls. "It was all very intense and competitive at the top junior level, but basically Mac had fewer problems calling his own lines than he does with linesman on the court today. He beat me 6–3, 6–4 that time with both of us playing from the backcourt. Mac was just kicking in his serve in those days. None of us had any serves to speak of."

By the time he was selected for the American Junior Davis Cup team at the age of sixteen, McEnroe was developing a serve and a lot more besides. Nonetheless, big national junior titles always eluded him. Although he won his fair share of doubles, the name of McEnroe is not to be found on the list of USTA junior singles champions, except on clay: not at the age of twelve, fourteen or even sixteen. Yet by eighteen, of course, he had made that quantum jump to the senior level and the dizzy heights of the Wimbledon semifinal.

Larry Gottfried, Brian's younger brother, was the boy who most frequently denied McEnroe those junior titles, and ironically Larry was one of the few top juniors of the era who never followed through to make it in the pro ranks. Apart from Teltscher, Van Winitsky, a good-looking, cocksure prankster who was always getting ragged by his teammates on the Junior Davis Cup squad for his boundless self-confidence, was another of McEnroe's great rivals and at that age one of his better friends. There were times when a long-suffering coach called Bill McGowan took this high-spirited group of Junior Davis Cup-pers—apart from McEnroe, Teltscher and Van Winitsky, Tony Giammalva, Robert Van t'Hof and Jay di Louie were also on board—on a nationwide tour, sometimes by plane and sometimes in a long limousine with seven or eight packed in the back. Heaven knows how they survived.

"We were a pretty wild bunch," admits Winitsky. "Once in a coffee shop in San Francisco the waitress eventually tore off her apron and stormed out after we had kept sending her back for one more glass of water. She just went bananas. I used to get the most shit from coach McGowan. Then, I suppose, it was McEnroe who got in the most trouble. We seemed to have a lot in common in those days, especially in music. He and I were into Deep Purple while Rennert liked Traffic."

McEnroe had already got a close-up look at the big world of professional tennis when he started ball-boying during the U.S. Open at Forest Hills.

"I ball-boyed for Ilana Kloss and Regina Marsikova when they were playing in the juniors—can you believe that?" McEnroe grinned. "And I ball-boyed when Pilic played Borg one year, and Nikki gave me a lot of shit. But it gave me a good chance to see how those guys played."

Although McEnroe quickly graduated to higher things, some of the kids who used to ball-boy with him are still at it. "They just enjoy being involved for a couple of weeks in the summer," McEnroe explains. "They work some of my matches now, and I'll suddenly remember their names as I turn around and say, 'Let's have that ball, Bruce.' It's sort of strange."

McEnroe first played at the U.S. Open when he was sixteen, partnering Tony Palafox in the doubles.

Ironically they were drawn against Vitas Gerulaitis and Peter Fleming, who had stepped in as a last-minute replacement for Sandy Mayer who was injured. So Palafox found himself on court with three players he had coached! It was not until a couple of years later that McEnroe and Fleming came together on the same side of the net. They played together in Los Angeles and San Francisco and did well enough—reaching the semifinal both times—to want to try again when McEnroe left Stanford. By 1978 they were in the Wimbledon final, and in 1979 they were champions. They may yet end up winning more major titles than any other pair in the history of the modern game.

After reaching the Wimbledon semifinal in 1977, there was much speculation in the press as to whether McEnroe would continue with his plan of going to Stanford University in northern California or would be seduced, at the age of eighteen, by the allure of the professional circuit and its amazing riches.

"But there was never any real doubt that he was going to go to college," says his father. "It was something he had been working for all his life, and even if he didn't stay for more than a year, we all felt it was important for him to get a taste of college life."

McEnroe agrees. "The good thing was that I had passed my entrance exams before doing well at Wimbledon, so I had the added incentive of not wanting to throw away all that work. I'm really glad I went. I had a really good time."

McEnroe started studying mathematics and calculus and initially signed up for a whole variety of subjects. But eventually, as it became apparent that professional tennis really was going to be his career, he searched around for something that did not require a great deal of written work. The emphasis had suddenly switched. Tennis had taken priority; tennis was work, and work, in the accepted sense, had been relegated to the role of an interesting pastime.

John relates, "Eventually I found this exposition class where the lady said 'no papers, no tests required, we're just going to talk.' So we just had to sit around and rap about things that bothered us, and it was good because some really weird things came out which taught us a lot about people.

"There was this guy who admitted for the first time in his life that he was a homosexual. Imagine doing that in front of twenty-five people! And then there was someone else who talked about a friend of his who had been mugged by a black man and somehow implied that mugging was a racial thing. There were two black girls in the class and one of them got really upset and stood up and said, 'My mother was raped by a white man and I'm the result.' Then she rushed out in tears. We all thought 'Oh, my God, what do we do now?' It was real heavy-duty stuff, man, I tell you. So we told the guy to go and apologize."

Under the tutelage of the well-respected Stanford coach Dick Gould, McEnroe was also continuing his education on the tennis court. Although John didn't put in as many hours on the practice court as teammates like Bill Maze, Matt Mitchell and his old pal Peter Rennert, Gould has nothing but praise for the way his No. 1 player conducted himself as a member of the team.

"A coach couldn't have asked for more," Gould told me. "Apart from being the finest all-around athlete I have ever had here he was also the greatest team player I have ever known. He always had a deep concern for the other guys. He would always take the time to console those who had lost and help them work on their games if they needed it.

"And his dedication was never in question. One occasion I remember especially occurred when we were in Austin, Texas, and had to drive down to San Antonio to play Trinity, where Larry Gottfried was No. 1. John wasn't feeling well and, in fact, was running a fever of 104 by the time we left. But he insisted on playing and went out there in front of a really hostile crowd and played his guts out and never lost his composure. And then he came back and played doubles, too. It was a really impressive effort."

But the pinnacle of achievement at Stanford as far as McEnroe was concerned came when he followed in the footsteps of Jimmy Connors (1971) and Billy Martin (1975) by winning the National Collegiate Amateur Athletic Championship in his freshman year. Held at the University of Georgia's Henry Field Stadium, the NCAA finals are a high point in any American tennis player's career, and veteran observers among the three thousand crowd on a blazingly hot June day in 1978 have rated McEnroe's 7–6, 7–6, 5–7, 7–6 victory over John Sadri, then a senior at North Carolina State, as the greatest college match they have ever seen. It lasted four hours and in the end only one point divided them on aggregate—McEnroe having won 144 to Sadri's 143.

It required all McEnroe's speed of eye and exquisite timing to blunt the ferocious power of Sadri's serve, which was already being talked of as one of the fastest in the game at any level. But John triumphed, ending his days in the younger echelons of tennis at the top of the heap. The length of time it had taken him to get there can, I think, be partially explained by the realization at Stanford that it was as a tennis player that he was going to be judged and that nothing else really mattered. As soon as he had made up his mind about that, all the fierce endeavor and compulsive competitive urge that had been evident in his varied activities as a child came to be focused on just one thing—his tennis.

There were beginning to be times, of course, when the fierceness of that effort boiled over, but some keen observers had never doubted his ability to channel that effort and that talent into an unwavering pursuit of excellence.

Tommy Tucker, one of the game's great enthusiasts who is now assistant director of tennis under Tom Gorman at the Mission Hills Country Club in Palm Springs, first noticed something extraordinary about McEnroe when he was fifteen. "I had never seen anyone reaching for perfection with such intensity," Tucker told me. "It was all in his face—the contortion, the pain, the effort. In a way I found it beautiful."

At about this time McEnroe was beginning to think about beauty of a different kind. Stacy Margolin was a contemporary on the junior circuit and became the first girl to catch and to hold his eye. "It was easy then," John recalled a little wistfully one day. "We were both just a couple of young players of about the same standard enjoying the same things. It got a little bit more complicated when we started playing different circuits."

But even then John went to extraordinary lengths to keep the relationship going, and despite a few inevitable problems created by the pressures of fame, Stacy remains the only girl who has meant anything permanent in his life. It is in many ways an unlikely partnership and one that is typical of the cosmopolitan tennis circuit. Through tennis, a New York Irish Catholic boy and a Beverly Hills Jewish girl, divided perhaps by more than a continent, have met and discovered things in common.

4

AN AUTUMN TOUR—AND
THE TALENT BLOSSOMS

After his first-round loss to Erik Van Dillen at Wimbledon, following his one year at college, McEnroe still had much to prove as he set out on a long tour of the Grand Prix circuit in the autumn of 1978. He had done well enough at the U.S. Open, dropping only one set on his way to the semifinal, where Jimmy Connors once again proved too experienced for him, winning with disdainful ease, 6–2, 6–2, 7–5.

Connors' victory seemed to confirm that the game's established hierarchy was not yet ready to let any nineteen-year-old upstart with a huge talent and hot temper muscle in on their jealously guarded perch at the top of the tennis world. Björn Borg and Jimmy Connors were the undisputed leaders of a familiar group of top-ten players which included Guillermo Vilas, Eddie Dibbs, Vitas Gerulaitis, Brian Gottfried, Raul Ramirez, Roscoe Tanner and Harold Solomon. Few experts had any doubt that John McEnroe would soon be in among them, but nobody was really prepared for the speed and the brilliance of the assault he was about to launch—an assault he would carry right around the world to bloody the game's acknowledged king at his own Swedish court.

Immediately after the U.S. Open at Flushing Meadow, McEnroe won his first Grand Prix singles title at a small event in Hartford, Connecticut. The news of that victory reached those of us attending the Arco Open in Los Angeles like a warning shot from the East. It seemed logical to assume that this would be the first of many. Within a week McEnroe was out west for the $175,000 TransAmerica Open in San Francisco, proving all his supporters right.

It was there, at the famous Cow Palace, scene of so many great political and sporting occasions, that I came to a personal decision about John Patrick McEnroe, Jr. Looking back, I suppose it was a farsighted attempt to preserve my sanity; and in a perverse sort of way, I have Jimmy Connors to thank for it. During the previous ten years, I had been driven to the brink of despair on numerous occasions by Con-

A thoughtful ATP president, Harold Solomon. Every year John McEnroe flies down to Florida to support Solly's Hunger Project charity exhibition. *Serge Philippot*

nors' behavior on court and his attitude off it. I was often unable to decide which appalled me more, having to watch his matches with his strutting, arrogant and often obscene acts of bravado, or his truly embarrassing performances in press conferences as he struggled to recognize the meaning of "defeat"—a word he had never been taught as a child.

I tried to concentrate on the brilliance of his tennis but always found it very difficult to ignore the rest. It is all much easier now, of course, because Jimmy has grown up, matured, got married to a wondrously beautiful girl and generally come to terms with the fact that being the second- or third-best tennis player in the world is really not all that bad. He has become at times an articulate spokesman for his sport and, as an entertainer who always gives his all, is worth his weight in gold.

But when I saw McEnroe appear on the horizon I thought, "Oh, God, here we go again!" I recognized the short-tempered, highly strung, intensely competitive signs that had been so apparent in Connors at the same age, and I didn't like what I saw. But equally I had no intention of spending the next ten years sitting in press conferences around the world watching a player whose behavior I didn't like and didn't understand. So, in San Francisco, I decided to do something about it. I decided to try to get to know this strange-looking and obviously intensely shy young man. I had never got to know Connors on a personal basis, which was hardly surprising because I had been highly critical of him in print and he, quite understandably, did not go out of his way to treat me as a friend.

In getting to know McEnroe, I knew that Peter Fleming was my best bet. Peter had already been on the circuit a couple of years, and we had become more than casual acquaintances during the previous two weeks because he had been kind enough to loan me his car. This proved to be a Datsun 240Z, which had been sitting in the bowels of a garage near the UCLA campus ever since he had left the university, and which was badly in need of some exercise. Actually it required quite a bit of exercise to drive the car—a powerful, snorting, wonderfully eccentric little monster that punished the driver noisily for any errors of timing with the clutch. In many ways it provided the best possible practice for getting to know John McEnroe.

But, in fact, I quickly found him much more agreeable off court than I had supposed. With Peter there to break the ice, he treated me with a great deal less suspicion than he would other adults trying to get too close. And, to my surprise, I soon discovered Fleming was right when he described John as "very mature for his age." I know that the on-court image is one of childishness and immaturity, but that is the performer wearing his performer's clothes. It is not a voluntary guise but a schizoid state common among many hypertense entertainers. Let me quote just one example—and one to whom McEnroe can certainly relate, given his love of rock music. The rock star Peter Frampton, discussing in a radio interview the transformation he undergoes on stage, said, "Basically I'm a quiet person, really quite shy, I suppose. But when I get on stage something takes hold of me and I change completely. I become a maniac."

Away from the competitive arena there was no doubt that McEnroe came across as a quiet, thoughtful and sensible young man who was very quick on the uptake. Not exactly what I had been led to expect. But Fleming had insisted this was so and he was right. The pair had first met at Port Washington when Peter was sixteen and John twelve. Before long they had become friends, and the age difference, usually considerable for boys in their teens, never seemed to matter very much. Peter calling McEnroe "Junior" was the only obvious outward sign that the pair were not exact contemporaries.

"It didn't take me long to find out how good he was," Peter told me when we talked about their first meeting some time later. "I looked at this twelve-year-old kid in the coffee shop at Port Washington and told him I'd give him five games a set. My game was OK, nothing amazing, you understand, but hell, I was four years older and I thought I'd be able to handle it. The best I did was 6–2. After that we began practicing together a lot. I mean, we must have played each other hundreds and hundreds of times. As you know, John is not big on practice but we always used to play for a couple of beers or dinner or something, and we played our guts out. He deliberately used to call me names and get me annoyed so as to get my competitive juices flowing. I think it was the only way he could make a practice match hold his interest. Intentionally or not, it sure helped me. I learned from him just by watching the way he competed. And then later, I think I probably helped him a bit by being around as a friend when he first came onto the tour. Not that he was slow to make friends with other players. He's always been pretty relaxed in the locker room. But we were especially close and still are."

With Borg and Gerulaitis as top seeds and Gottfried, Dibbs and Tanner as backup cast, promoter Barry McKay, the former U.S. Davis Cup player and Kramer touring pro, would have been more than satisfied with his field in San Francisco. But even before the talented South African Andrew Pattison upset Borg in the third round, McEnroe was attracting an inordinate amount of attention for a No. 8 seed. David Schneider, another South African, with a lopsided grin and a restless curiosity about the world, came nearest to causing McEnroe real stress in the early rounds by forcing him into a third-set tie-break. But after that the group of Stanford University friends who came up each night from nearby Palo Alto to cheer their hero were given few worries as McEnroe's lethal serving disposed of three tour veterans, Marty Riessen, Kim Warwick and Adriano Panatta, without the loss of a set. Little Eddie Dibbs, one of the game's great unsung humorists, didn't find much to laugh about as McEnroe's incredible variety of skills edged him out of a tense battle, 6–4, 7–6.

"I mean, what can I say?" shrugged Dibbs afterward, looking as if the dog he'd backed at his favorite Miami racetrack had just fallen on its nose. "The kid's amazing. He's got all this stuff coming at you from everywhere and he's quick, I'll tell you that, he's quick."

In the final, McEnroe appeared to be in deep trouble as another experienced campaigner, Dick Stockton, a Wimbledon semifinalist in 1974, produced a near-perfect illustration of serve-and-volley tennis during the first two sets. For the first hour Stockton was finding the mark with 82 percent of his first serves, and it was only the fighting qualities he displayed in winning the second-set tie-break by 7 points to 5 that saved McEnroe from defeat. After that, Stockton went off the boil and McEnroe claimed his first important Grand Prix title by 2–6, 7–6, 6–2.

In the press conference McEnroe showed that he could analyze a match with as much precision as he could play it. "Tennis is all about momentum," observed McEnroe accurately. "There is no doubt that

Peter Fleming, the giant from New Jersey who is McEnroe's confidant, friend and doubles partner, looks happy enough in the Jamaican sunshine, although ironically it was there during the WCT Challenge Cup in 1979 that he had one of his few rows with McEnroe. "He just pissed me off when we played each other—you know the way he can sometimes," said Peter. "But we sat down and had a little talk about it. He's pretty cool about criticism when it comes from a friend."

Dick should have won in straight sets. Until the tie-break I was having trouble getting his first serve back over the net. Then suddenly I started moving better. I felt I could hit the ball again. And as soon as I was able to put some pressure on him, he started to make mistakes. It's hard to serve like he was for three sets."

Unlike a lot of cities in America, San Francisco does actually have some sportswriters who know one end of a tennis racket from the other. But even for those who still insisted on calling a rally a volley—oh, you'd be surprised how many still do—that little critical summation by the new TransAmerica champion should have told them all they needed to know.

While I headed back to Santa Monica to wrestle with Allen Fox's book and Peter Fleming's Datsun Z, McEnroe sharpened his skills in two smaller Grand Prix events: first, on the Hawaiian island of Maui, where he lost to the eventual winner, Bill Scanlon, in the semifinal, and then all the way over to Switzerland, where Guillermo Vilas beat him in the final at Basle. It was time for the next Super Series event on his schedule, the Stockholm Open—a tournament that had, during its comparatively brief nine-year-history, earned the reputation of being one of the best run in the world.

Even before Nikki Pilic won the first Stockholm Open in 1969, the famous Kunglihallen on the outskirts of that charming city had been a breeding ground for some of Europe's great indoor champions. Players like Lennart Bergelin, now Borg's coach, Sven Davidson, Jan-Erik Lundquist and Ulf Schmidt had all played much of their formative tennis there, as, indeed, had Borg himself. But if the special tiled courts—a surface unique, in my experience, to the Kunglihallen—had always been fast, they were certainly getting no slower with age. This was partially the reason why Borg, already a three-time winner at Wimbledon, had never been able to win his local event.

As soon as I saw the way the tiles reacted to McEnroe's serve, I knew it would take something special to stop him joining the long list of American success stories in Stockholm. Serve-and-volley experts like Arthur Ashe, Stan Smith, Tom Gorman and Sandy Mayer had all carried off little replicas of the Skandia Cup to place on their trophy-laden mantelpieces. Sure enough, McEnroe did not take long to join them. Tom Okker, still a sprightly and dangerous opponent, gave him pause in a closely fought second-set tie-break, but no one else came as near to taking a set off him—certainly not poor Tim Gullikson who got crushed 6–2, 6–2 in the final.

But, of course, it was McEnroe's semifinal defeat of Björn Borg by the entirely deserving margin of 6–3, 6–4 that left Sweden dumbstruck. The match made front-page news the entire length of the country, and one could almost hear television sets in Lapland freeze over and reindeer drop icy tears as the severity of the defeat became known. It was not just the fact that their national hero had lost that shocked the Swedes. The tennis experts among them had been aware of the possibility because the speed of the court so obviously favored McEnroe's game. But for Borg to lose in one hour and fourteen minutes without ever seeming capable of offering any real resistance was almost humiliating.

But neither the Swedish press nor, indeed, Borg himself attempted to offer any excuses. There really weren't any to make. "McEnroe was, to be honest, never in any trouble at all," wrote Björn Hellberg in the *Slazenger Year Book.* "So strong was the American's serve that Borg—regarded as the best returner in the game—only got seven points against it in the entire match!"

A disappointed Borg was philosophical. "There was little I could do," he said. "John just played too well for me."

Interestingly it was the first time that Borg, himself a teenage wonder, had lost to a player younger than himself. Their future matches would rarely be as one-sided, but the decisiveness of that first victory was important for McEnroe, as it gave him a little psychological armor for the battles that lay ahead.

And so to London. The Benson & Hedges Championships, now so much a part of the winter sporting scene, was a mere two years old when McEnroe made his first appearance at Wembley. The tournament might have been young, but, like the Kunglihallen, the old arena was rich in tennis history, as well as being the home of so many other sports. I first saw Pancho Segura there, illuminating the old London Professional Championships with his bowlegged, double-fisted brilliance. I saw Lew Hoad take a set off the other Pancho—Gonzales—6–0 in thirteen minutes on the fast boards that they used in those days. But Hoad secured only the first set; Gonzales won the other two. And it was at one of those bars behind the restaurant that a young Mike Davies, full of Welsh fire and visionary enthusiasm, bought me a beer back in 1961 as he outlined his dreams for professional tennis. Later, as executive director of World Championship Tennis, he made some of them come true.

There had been doubts about bringing top-class tennis back to Wembley, which is not the most central location in the London area. But Benson & Hedges are five-star sponsors, and when Jimmy Connors won the first tournament and Björn Borg the second, a new tradition had been born. In 1978, with neither Connors nor Borg present, the event badly needed a drawing card to maintain the level of interest. John McEnroe arrived just in time.

David Lloyd, Tom Okker, Corrado Barazzutti and Dick Stockton were swept aside without the loss of a set, but in the final, facing the determined Tim Gullikson for the second straight week, McEnroe found himself seriously challenged for the first time since losing to Vilas in Basle.

Tom, the left-handed of the Gullikson twins, utilized to full effect the great strength of his game, the return of serve, and won the first set on the tie-break, but not before McEnroe, exploding with rage and indignation, had threatened to walk off court after a bad umpiring mistake. On the first set-point to Gullikson in the tie-break, Tom went for a backhand down the line, and the ball actually hit the net-cord judge before falling between the tramlines. Apparently the umpire wasn't looking because he gave the set to Gullikson. Even though the mistake was obvious, it took two or three minutes of shouting on McEnroe's part before the umpire, after consulting his linespeople, got the message and reversed his decision.

The fit McEnroe threw was not a pretty sight, but would justice have been better served if he had politely said, "Excuse me, but I think there has been an error," and been ignored? Was yelling and screaming the only way to get things put right? One would like to think not, but I must confess that I am far from sure.

As it turned out it became immaterial because Gullikson won the tie-break fair and square four points later and a large audience was

Tom Gullikson, the left-handed twin, pouring a celebration drink for his brother Tim. *Syndication International*

treated to a ruggedly contested feast of serve-and-volley tennis, with McEnroe's greater range of skills gradually gaining the upper hand to win the last three sets 6–4, 7–6, 6–2.

"If I win, I'll treat you to dinner," McEnroe had promised me before the match. Although his tastes are a mite more sophisticated now, his idea of a good meal at the age of nineteen was a double helping of the best hamburger at Wolfie's in Park Lane. That was fair enough, because, as he and Peter had won the doubles, it was a double celebration. Although his fame was spreading, he still wasn't as well known as he is today, but he was certainly known at Wolfie's. He had been cleaning out the kitchen there most of the week, judging by the reception he received from the tall, shapely waitresses. In that respect he was behaving like the typical tennis pro. If they find a place they like, they turn it into a substitute home for the week—quite a natural reaction for people who are constantly on the move.

In the five weeks since San Francisco, McEnroe had been on the move in more senses than one. He had been moving up the ATP computer so fast that even Borg and Connors were beginning to feel the draft. It would be a while before he would actually overtake either of them, but based on what I had witnessed on the tour that autumn, I had no hesitation in writing in the December 9 issue of *Tennis Week:* "In my opinion John McEnroe is currently the best tennis player in the world." It was an evaluation based, of course, on who was playing the best tennis at that particular stage of the year. There was no question of suggesting that he deserved the No. 1 ranking, because that can only be earned by a player winning at least one of the Grand Slam titles. But from September to December 1978, I had not seen anyone come near to emulating McEnroe's record of consistency or rivaling the sheer brilliance of his play.

I did not base my judgment just upon his annihilation of Borg in Stockholm, although that proved beyond doubt that he was not afraid of reputations. I was more convinced by the fact that I had never seen any player come straight out of the college ranks and begin *routinely* beating hardened, high-ranking tour veterans in straight sets week after week: Stockton, Okker, Panatta, Dibbs, Riessen, Tim Gullikson—these were no pushover opponents. But this young man was pushing them to one side as if he was in a hurry to get up to the very top of the mountain in one great leap.

Actually McEnroe was remarkably realistic and patient about the amount of time it would take him to do that, and it is another major plus for his character that he was never a bragger or a boaster. He was never one to lay claim to something he did not genuinely feel was his. So he knew it would take time. But the start he made in the autumn of 1978 left me in no doubt at all that, probably sooner than later, he would indeed be recognized as the best tennis player in the world.

5

1979—A YEAR OF CONSOLIDATION

The following twelve months removed the final doubts, if any remained, concerning John McEnroe's quality. By the time he had won the Masters in January 1979, the WCT Dallas finals in May, and the U.S. Open in September, no one needed any more convincing that he was the twenty-four-carat genuine article—a true world-class champion, not merely by virtue of his amazing virtuosity with a racket, but also because of that other vital ingredient, the ability to win under pressure.

Wimbledon, of course, remained a special problem after his surprising fourth-round loss to none other than Tim Gullikson. But that apart, he had become the third force in the Borg-Connors-McEnroe triumvirate that won everything that really mattered during the course of the year and a lot else besides.

His rise had been swift and spectacular in his utter domination of the rank and file. It is an old adage in tennis that every player needs a killer shot to become a champion. But it would be simplifying the issue to pick on one shot out of McEnroe's vast and varied armory. Rather it is the actual variety that is so stunning. A player who possesses such an array of available options automatically puts fearful pressure on his opponent. What is he going to do next? The question eats away at the back of the mind, eroding the most carefully drawn-up tactical plan and withering the will. It is not by shouting and complaining that McEnroe wins the all-important and so often overlooked psychological battles that are always raging unseen out there on court in a top-class professional match, but simply by tactically preventing his opponent from playing the way he wants. Although his own pavonine skills, often so arrogantly and effortlessly brilliant, tend to capture all the attention, they frequently act as a smokescreen for the tactical ploys that are slowly but surely dismantling the other man's game.

It is because McEnroe is so intensely involved in this all-encompassing physical and psychological warfare that he has no time for the

Left: After losing to him twice indoors the previous winter, Tim Gullikson acknowledges the cheers from his Wimbledon fans after beating a despondent McEnroe on No. 2 Court in 1979. *Syndication International*

Below: Mac of the London *Daily Mail* wryly recorded Tim Gullikson's defeat of McEnroe. *Syndication International*

'Of course I'm a little disappointed but Gullikson played well and there's always next year . . .'

niceties of acknowledging a good shot from the other side of the net. Instantly McEnroe is blaming himself for having *allowed* his opponent to get into a position from which he was able to unleash the winning forehand or backhand lob. The fact that the man he is playing can hit shots of equal power and brilliance is not the issue as far as McEnroe is concerned. He knows that, and is more than ready to acknowledge it before or after the match. As soon as battle commences, McEnroe becomes totally engrossed in the task of preventing those shots from hurting him. And when they do, the pain can be seen in his face. And yet he is not really thinking about the ball that just flew past him for a spectacular winner. His mind has already locked onto the ball *he* hit. Obviously it was too fast or too slow or not accurate enough—hence the self-recrimination.

That kind of reaction will not be seen, however, if Borg latches on to his best serve wide to the ad court and smacks it back down the line for a winner. That was McEnroe's best effort and Borg's best effort. Too tough. McEnroe has no problem with that. So, in a sense, he is a spoiler. Players, especially players he has met often and really studied, come off court knowing that he has not allowed them to play. Only a man with a wide variety of skills can do that. But, of course, he needs the big weapons too, and in McEnroe's case I would have to pick on the serve and the ability to do almost anything he wants with a volley that make him, at times, virtually unplayable. The feel and timing he possesses are quite remarkable. I have never seen anyone quite so adept at being able to turn the most blistering return into a featherweight drop volley.

Nevertheless it is interesting that coach Palafox picks on the volley as one of the few areas for criticism in John's game. "He is in to the net so fast that sometimes, with the forehand grip, he has no time to adjust," Palafox points out. "So he hits up because he is lacking that fraction of a second to set himself right."

It was Palafox, incidentally, who taught McEnroe to ease up on crucial points and resist the temptation to hit the ball too hard. "As a junior he had a tendency to go for the big shot at 15–40. I stopped that. He still likes to hit the ball harder in doubles, and that is correct because there is more chance of someone intercepting in a limited space. But in singles he likes to move people around and do more things with the ball."

It was chance, however, and not Palafox that taught McEnroe his unique serve. "I suppose I was already a little bit sideways on because that seemed sort of natural for a left-hander," John explained. "But the action I have today really evolved when I was eighteen. I had a back problem and was wearing a brace when I played Erik Van Dillen at the

U.S. Open. I wasn't comfortable with it so I took it off and started bending forward really low just before I served so as to loosen the back muscles.

"Quite by accident I found that the movement pulled me round to an even more sideways stance. Then, as I continued the muscle-loosening exercise every time I served in other matches, I started to notice that I could hit better angles and that people were having a tougher time reading each delivery. So, even though the back is fine, and I don't need to bend low anymore, I decided to keep the service action just as it was."

Ironically it was not his lethal serve that carried McEnroe to the first major title of his fledgling career at Madison Square Garden in January 1979. The serve, in fact, was the least impressive part of his game as he hung on to beat Arthur Ashe, whose career was to be so cruelly cut short just a few months later. Incredibly McEnroe had allowed the first set to slip from his grasp when he served three consecutive double faults with the score standing at 5–4, 40–love. Ashe peered querulously through his contact lenses at his young opponent and quickly accepted the gift, winning the set on the tie-break. Having lost the second 3–6, Ashe actually led 4–1 in the decider before McEnroe's fighting qualities were put to their first real test in a crunch situation, and they did not fail him as the native New Yorker showed the pro-Ashe crowd of seventeen thousand just what he could do by reeling off five straight games for victory.

It was not a vintage Masters. With Borg, Vilas and Gerulaitis all boycotting the event in another of the game's petty feuds, there was never much chance of that. And even McEnroe's first-ever victory over Connors was robbed of much of its significance by the fact that Jimmy was forced to retire with a badly blistered foot at 0–3 down in the second set. But even allowing for Connors' handicap, one detected the first signs that McEnroe was learning how to handle an opponent who had completely dominated him in the past. He was discovering how to put the handcuffs on his tormentor. A few months later he would have Jimmy well and truly under lock and key.

But a Masters title was proof of that quality, certainly proof enough for John Barrett, who wrote in the *Slazenger Year Book*, ". . . he has proved beyond doubt that his technique, his skill with a racket, his speed of thought and movement and, above all, his courage and will to win are of the highest order. The $500,000 he has won in his seven months as a professional has been earned on merit alone. Forget about luck, forget about the absence of certain players. Concentrate instead on his ability and recognize him for what he is: a worthy successor to Laver, Ashe, Connors and Borg."

McEnroe with the WCT New Orleans singles trophy and tournament director Peter Curtis, the former British Davis Cup player. *Russ Adams*

Czech star Tomas Smid—a McEnroe victim in the WCT New Orleans quarterfinals, and again in the Davis Cup quarters at Flushing Meadow the week after John won Wimbledon. *Richard Evans*

But, having skipped the Masters, Borg was waiting for his new rival on the WCT tour just a few weeks later. In the semifinal at Richmond, Virginia, Björn survived a hair-raising second-set tie-break, eventually winning it by 10 points to 8 after McEnroe had reached match point four times. By all accounts, Borg's 4–6, 7–6, 6–3 victory remains one of their most dramatic and brilliantly fought battles, but it was rivaled a month later when McEnroe turned the tables in New Orleans at another WCT event promoted by the former British player Peter Curtis. It was a memorable week in many ways, not least for the fact that Ilie Nastase actually got thrown off court in the third set of his first-round match with Bob Lutz. After that uproar died down, we were treated to some superb tennis. The Czech, Tomas Smid, sharpened McEnroe's game for him in the quarters before going down in three hard-fought sets, and that set the stage for another semifinal showdown with Borg. After being completely outplayed in the second set, Borg tested the younger man's nerve and skill to the nth degree in the third as he forced the match into the deciding tie-break. But once again McEnroe proved he could stand the pressure as he came up with some lethal serves and acrobatic volleys to clinch a 5–7, 6–1, 7–6 victory. After that Roscoe Tanner was swept aside in straight sets in the final, 6–4, 6–2—a sudden reversal of fortunes for Roscoe, who had beaten McEnroe with comparative ease in the quarters of the U.S. Pro Indoors in Philadelphia just a few weeks before. But McEnroe was growing in stature week by week now, and although he and Peter Fleming had already won the WCT Braniff World Doubles title in London at the beginning of the year, New Orleans provided him with his first WCT singles crown and it proved to be a good omen for Dallas.

But there was some traveling to be done before his rendezvous at high noon in the Big D. Twenty-four hours after beating Tanner in New Orleans, John McEnroe was in Milan, a city that, after London, is as familiar to him as any in the world outside the United States. McEnroe's Italian connection really came about as a result of his close and somewhat unlikely friendship with a feisty little ex-player called Sergio Palmieri. Tough and resourceful, Palmieri is not afraid to make himself unpopular in pursuit of something he believes to be right—and in that, of course, he shares common ground with McEnroe.

Although he was a somewhat controversial director of the Italian Open for a couple of years, it is as right-hand man to two of the most successful personalities in Italian tennis, Sergio Tacchini and Carlo della Vida, that Palmieri's hard-driving talents have been best employed. A contemporary of Palmieri's as a player, Tacchini quickly built his clothing company into a top-line name in tennis fashions and, like his rivals Fila and later Ellesse, recognized the need to have his shirts on the backs of the best players in the world. So, as a Tacchini rep at the French Open in 1977, Palmieri was naturally interested in all the promising newcomers competing at Stade Roland Garros that year.

"The problem was, the first time we met I didn't recognize him," laughed Sergio. "I don't think he was too pleased. He was wearing Fila clothes then, and Marty Mulligan, who was working for both Fila and Diadora shoes at the time, dropped a pair of shoes round at my booth for John to pick up. When I returned to the booth later in the day I saw this guy standing there asking for shoes and I said, 'Who are you?' Eh, bellissimo, such a good start. But we get on better after that."

So much better, in fact, that after Palmieri had shown McEnroe the confidence he had in him by inviting him in 1978 to play in an exhibition in Milan with Borg, Gerulaitis and Panatta—starry-eyed company for a youngster still at college—Sergio became McEnroe's main business contact and closest European friend. Naturally a Tacchini contract was waiting for him as soon as he left Stanford, and McEnroe, while still shying away from the rigors of the red clay at the Foro Italico in Rome, nevertheless became a regular visitor to the two major indoor events that Palmieri runs in Milan each year for della Vida, one of Europe's best promoters of sporting events.

When I spoke to Palmieri recently in New York he told me, "Since 1978, he has never missed one of our tournaments. That's seven times now he has played in Milan. Of course, he makes good money in the exhibition and it's good business for us, too. But we never talk about business too much when we are together. But I know he is interested in money. He always wants to know how we are making out at the tournament and things like that. But mostly we just relax between his matches and have a good time. He stays at my place in Milan—my cleaning lady, she is not too happy about that: socks, rackets, clothes, such a mess. And we have special restaurants he likes to eat at. Sometimes I take him to the Santa Luccia where all the Milanese theater people go, but mostly he prefers a quieter place called Torre del Manga where the food is also fantastic. It is typical he prefers the place where he can relax out of the limelight, and, of course, they are very good to us there, staying open after closing time when he has a late match."

Whether it was the food, the company or the general efficiency of the whole setup at the Palazzo dello Sport, McEnroe quickly felt at home, and his tennis reflected his happy frame of mind right from the start. Crushing Gerulaitis 6–0, 6–3 in the semis and encountering only marginally more resistance from Australian veteran John Alexander in the final, McEnroe won the Ramazzotti Cup, which was then a combined

WCT/Grand Prix event, in style. Although he was to have his ups and downs in the exhibitions that followed much later each year, he was to retain the Cup in 1980, beating Vijay Amritraj in the final, and again in 1981 with one of his most decisive victories over Borg.

In 1979, however, Borg got the better of McEnroe on the next stop of the WCT tour in Rotterdam by beating him 6–4, 6–2 in a rather disappointing final. But the young New Yorker had, of course, done more than enough to qualify for the eight-man field in Dallas. Although Borg had won three WCT titles to his two, McEnroe actually finished on top of the points table by virtue of having played in Philadelphia where greater prize money earned double points. Could McEnroe justify being top man in a field in Dallas that included Borg, Connors, Gerulaitis and Tanner? Results at the Alan King Classic at Caesar's Palace Hotel in Las Vegas the previous week raised doubts about that. Playing under lights on a balmy desert night, McEnroe had once again failed to handle Connors' aggressive stroke play in a semifinal full of spectacular shotmaking and had gone down 7–5, 6–4. Borg, extending a winning streak to seventeen matches, then crowned himself the new Caesar by beating Connors in the final.

But a whole different wheel of fortune was awaiting them in Dallas. McEnroe opened with a 6–4, 6–0, 6–2 drubbing of John Alexander, who promptly announced in the press conference that McEnroe was as good as anyone he had ever played. "And I include Laver, Newcombe, Borg and Connors in that assessment," Alexander added.

The words had a prophetic ring because in the semis Connors suddenly discovered that he no longer held the whip hand over this shrewd and tenacious competitor who had finally got the "How to Beat Connors" manual fixed firmly in his head. Keeping Jimmy under constant pressure with the brilliance of his serving, the New Yorker mixed patience and steadiness from the backcourt with darting sorties to the net. And he always deprived Connors of the pace he craves. The score was 6–1, 6–4, 6–4 and it was as decisive as it sounds. With that psychological barrier lifted, McEnroe was mentally ready for yet another battle with Borg. In the end it was probably mental freshness that decided the issue, coupled with the unrelenting accuracy of McEnroe's wide, swinging serve into the ad court. Borg had played a little more tennis than he would have liked going into Dallas—he had won Monte Carlo before flying straight to Las Vegas—and the steely determination that he carries with him on court was just a fraction flimsier than usual. So the hungrier man got his deserts after an absorbing duel by 7–5, 4–6, 6–2, 7–6, and afterward Borg said of the new champion, "To play John, you must always play at the very top of your game." Coming from Björn, that was the ultimate compliment.

Harry Hopman, the Australian coach who helped McEnroe in his formative years and then came to his aid in 1981 by vetoing the $5,000 Wimbledon fine, takes some of the weight as his former pupil lifts the huge WCT trophy after beating Björn Borg in the 1979 Dallas finals. Former British No. 1 Mike Davies, then the executive director of WCT, is on the left. *Russ Adams*

So, within the space of five months, McEnroe had won the two big play-off finals of the world's circuit, and if his success at the Masters had proved primarily that he could seize his luck and win when he was playing below his best, the well-heeled, tennis-wise crowd of Texans who packed Moody Coliseum was left in no doubt as to McEnroe's ability to raise his game to just whatever level was required against the very best players in the world. Not since Ashe's memorable triumph at Wimbledon in 1975 had anyone beaten both Borg and Connors in the same tournament. That in itself was a significant achievement but McEnroe—no Muhammad Ali—was not getting carried away.

"No, I don't think I'm the No. 1 player in the world," he told the usual large assortment of international press that WCT invites to Dallas every year. "It's great to beat Connors and Borg, but I've got a lot to do before I can regard myself as No. 1. I mean, I haven't even won a Grand Slam title yet."

But it wouldn't be long. By September I was writing this report in *Tennis Week:*

After the racket had been flung in the air; the speeches made and the interviews given; after the hugs and handshakes and the very private conversation with father in a corner of the locker room, John McEnroe paused as he struggled into a crumpled pair of white jeans and said, "Jesus, I can't believe I just won the U.S. Open. . . . I mean, the *U.S. Open,* man, can you believe that?"

Sure. McEnroe's 7–5, 6–3, 6–3 over Vitas Gerulaitis, his clinical straight-set destruction of defending champion Jimmy Connors in the semifinal and his victory in the doubles with Peter Fleming—all this was merely a confirmation of what some of us had realized some time ago. Winning a major title—and winning it soon—was in this young man's stars. Nothing was going to stop him. The talent was too huge; the will too strong.

By winning the U.S. Open at the age of twenty, McEnroe had become the youngest player to wear that coveted crown since Pancho Gonzales in 1948. Now another young firebrand had seized control of American tennis, but if there were similarities in temperament between the two champions, the thirty-one years separating their individual triumphs had seen the U.S. Championships undergo an incredible metamorphosis: from all-amateur to open; from the West Side Tennis Club at Forest Hills to the National Tennis Center at Flushing Meadow; from patrician crowds drawn from country club and other exclusive bastions of the game to the howling, drunken mob of New York sports fans who descended on Flushing Meadow the night—that infamous Thursday night—when McEnroe played Nastase. These were changes that had made the game unrecognizable and unpalatable to many. But reality was no longer clothed in long white flannels. Gene Scott got it right when he wrote in *Tennis Week:*

We have entered a new era of spectator tennis. And those who insist we return to the fans of yesteryear with jackets and ties and "excuse me's" after an audible cough are out of touch. Professional football, baseball and [ice] hockey have had raucous scenes in the stands for years. Fighting and violence on and off the field are commonplace—however distasteful we find it.

In the wild growth we have encouraged for our sport in the past decade, there is a sort of rage inherent in the process. We have created a fire-breathing dragon and can't now retreat from harnessing her destructive force and presiding over her ultimate taming.

Certainly some taming was required after the scenes that erupted on that Thursday night when the idea of the game's two great bad boys meeting in the second round attracted a drunken, boorish crowd that gave tennis an unwelcome taste of just how some New York sports fans like to spend their evenings. In the end, after the spectators and officials had managed to turn the whole thing into a pantomime of the absurd, the two players were virtually turned into innocent bystanders.

True, Nastase and, to a lesser extent, McEnroe had knocked out a rough draft, whipped up a bit of enthusiasm and set the stage. But after that, people who were supposed to be nothing more than the supporting cast stole the show.

Frank Hammond, a Falstaffian figure in the chair, forgot all his best lines in the scene entitled "Big Match Crowd Control" and not only overreacted to Nastase but then completely blew his cool with the spectators. Mike Blanchard, a gentle and elderly referee, got into the act when matters started to deteriorate rather rapidly at 2–1 in the fourth set, with McEnroe leading by two sets to one. Hammond had accused Nastase of stalling and had started docking him penalty points and then an entire game when he refused to face McEnroe's serve. By this time the crowd, which had caused Nastase to stall in the first place, upped its noise level to ear-splitting proportions. Blanchard, still believing in sweet reason and common decency and all those other phrases that so many New Yorkers were never taught in English class, first tried to address them through a malfunctioning microphone and then, fumbling about with a ladder in an attempt to reach up to Hammond's mike, was lucky he didn't complete the farce by falling off.

By that time Billy Talbert, the tournament director, had enlarged the growing cast by walking on court, ignoring Hammond's clearly announced default of Nastase which had occurred moments earlier, and ordering Blanchard to take over from Frank in the chair. With ten thousand people making as long and as shrill a demonstration of sustained anger and abuse as I have ever heard in a sports arena, it was quite impossible to play tennis. So, despite all the command and countercommands from officials who were running around like chickens with their heads off, the two players just stood there looking more than a mite bewildered at the way their little play was panning out.

By their own standards, which aren't too terrific, I admit, neither Nastase nor McEnroe had done anything very bad, and the real tragedy was that during the first two sets they had produced tennis that was often breathtaking in its beauty. But all that had evaporated as the spectators seized on every little grimace and glance, every gesture of annoyance or line-call query, to force a confrontation and create what they had come for—a full-scale horror show. That they got it was their fault and the officials' fault. But, of course, there was no denying that a couple of tennis players called Nastase and McEnroe also played their part.

The spectators were never that bad again, but neither were they sweetness and light, especially as far as their two local heroes— McEnroe and Gerulaitis—were concerned. So it was poetic justice that, having spent most of the fortnight cheering the opponents of those players, they should end up with a final that would force them to cheer for one or the other. I have always found it the ultimate hypoc-

risy for New York crowds to boo John McEnroe for his behavior. McEnroe's behavior is New York behavior. Putting aside his Irish temper, the rough edges to his personality are pure New York, the result of too many rides on the subway with the elbow-jabbers and seat-snatchers and the strangers on the bus who let the door slam in your face—or worse. A nice, harmonious home in the suburbs doesn't eliminate the inevitable assimilation of that kind of behavior, that very real need to stand up and fight back before you get trampled to death.

So the U.S. Open crowds at Flushing Meadow in 1979 got the final they deserved and, perversely, it was more than some of them deserved. Beginning as the dying embers of a glorious September day threw an orange glow over the Manhattan skyline and finishing in the floodlit glare that had worried Björn Borg, the match was never close enough to be a classic. But Gerulaitis should derive some comfort from the fact that he participated in a duel rich in the game's finest skills.

Responding at last, the crowd was often left gasping at the sheer speed and athletic ability of the two men as they chased and parried, lunged and recovered both balance and composure in time to play yet another shot of perfect length and direction. But, hard though he tried, Vitas could never find a chink in McEnroe's armor. Was there one? Not apparently, with McEnroe playing to his full potential on the medium-paced composite surface called Decoturf. The firm footing gave him an even better springboard than usual from which to launch himself into the attack behind his serve; and for most of the match, he was hitting his first volley closer to the net than anyone I have ever seen, save, perhaps, for John Newcombe at his best. He was returning serve brilliantly, too, forcing Vitas to dig heavily topspun returns out from around his ankles. Despite the older man's great speed and dexterity, it was all too much for him, and long before the end it had become apparent that the boy from Douglaston would make the short drive home that night as the new champion of the United States.

But the triumphs did not stop there. Before he helped his country retain the Davis Cup with a crushing victory over Italy in San Francisco in December, McEnroe had already passed that way, stamping his name on the TransAmerica trophy he had won the year before. Then, as if confirmation was needed that his was as rare and as special a talent as tennis had seen at any stage of its history, he flew off to Stockholm and London and retained those Super Series titles as well. All in all, it had been a very good year.

Opposite: Vitas Gerulaitis and French friend at a Paris disco the year that the New Yorker reached the semifinal of the French Open. On the dance floor, McEnroe concedes, Vitas is definitely No. 1. *Rex Features*

6

SUMMERS IN THE
SOUTH OF FRANCE

"Say hello to the guys in Vichy," he said as I left him, shirtless, in the burning Provence sun, squatting on the steps of a grand old hotel in Aix. John McEnroe was the best under-21 player in the world in the summer of 1979, and I was heading north to Vichy where the Galea Cup, the world's premier under-21 team competition, was already in progress. McEnroe, tapping out a beat to an Eddie Money cassette, was waiting for the other members of the group, Jimmy Connors, Ilie Nastase, Guillermo Vilas and their various aides, mothers and agents, to finish lunch. Then they would travel on to Cap d'Agde and Pierre Barthes' mammoth fifty-court tennis camp for the third and final leg of an exhibition tour that would net this high-priced quartet more money in a week than any of the Galea Cup competitors had seen in their lives.

Nevertheless, just for a fleeting second, I thought I detected a hint of regret in McEnroe's voice—that instinctive reaction to the challenge of real competition, the compulsive desire to prove oneself. Looking back now, I am sure I was not mistaken. For a start, the players at Vichy that year, players like Ivan Lendl, Yannick Noah and Pascale Portes, were far closer to his age group than his colleagues on the "Carré d'As" exhibition tour, although ironically Vilas turned out to be a far better friend in later years than Lendl, with whom, at the time of this writing, McEnroe has a running feud.

But there was also the attraction of representing one's country in a meaningful competition—the thought of which certainly stirred McEnroe's interest almost as much as just making money. But as far as the Galea Cup is concerned, that was never a possibility because the USTA has never seen fit to enter a team. The fact that the United States is the only leading tennis nation that doesn't would appear to offer sufficient evidence of the stupidity of that decision, and the USTA is merely depriving its own young players of the chance to compete in an event that, alongside the Orange Bowl in Miami, ranks as the best junior tournament in the world. With the final rounds played over the best of five sets with no tie-breakers on slow red clay, the Galea Cup provides the best possible testing ground for a young player's stamina and ability to withstand pressure.

Had McEnroe—and a great many other Americans, for that matter—spent a couple of summers in Vichy, he might have taken a great deal less time to adapt to the technical and psychological demands of those courts at Stade Roland Garros where, at least prior to 1982, his hopes of winning the French Open lay buried.

As it was, McEnroe had started to spend a brief part of each summer in France, but in the south of France—Nice, Fréjus, Aix-en-Provence and Cap d'Agde, a mixture of the old and the new as far as tennis tradition was concerned. Although the big money exhibition tour was played in places that were either new for tennis but old for other things—like the Roman amphitheater at Fréjus—or just plain new, like the vast Exhibition Hall in Nice, the whole area is as resonant as any in the world with memories for virtually every leading player that the game has known since World War I.

In summers long gone, the courts of the Côte-d'Azur had been filled with figures like Suzanne Lenglen and Elizabeth Ryan, with a youthful Teddy Tinling in attendance as both player and umpire. King Gustav of Sweden was an active enthusiast, and apart from the five-year hiatus for World War II, the world's top players kept on coming, as they still do every spring for Grand Prix events in Nice and Monte Carlo.

It remains, despite Le Fast Food and Les Traffic Jams, a very special part of the world, and in the years to come I imagine it will retain a special place in John McEnroe's memory because, for one week each August, it has provided him with the opportunity to pause and reflect while playing tennis and earning money at the same time. Not a bad combination.

Each year, of course, he has returned a little wiser—although not necessarily any closer to solving his problems—and his visit in 1981 was particularly pleasant because he invited his mother ("I thought it was about time I gave her a holiday"), and it gave the pair of them more time to spend together over quiet and delicious dinners than at any previous period of his young adulthood.

But it was two years before, on his first trip in 1979, that I saw him in Aix. In less than a month he would win the U.S. Open for the first time and establish beyond further argument his credentials as one of the great players of his era. But that year, in particular, his week in the south of France offered him a chance for experimentation and introspection.

The matches on that leg of the tour were being played at the famous tennis club just outside Aix under the direction of Max Guerin, whose Raquet d'Or tournament had been thrown out of the Grand Prix the previous year in a fruitless and quite unfair attempt to make an example of someone suspected of committing the widespread crime of paying top players under-the-counter guarantees. Max's response was to give the tennis establishment a great big sad Gallic shrug and promptly to join forces with the show business promoters who were sponsoring the Carré d'As, which was much frowned upon by the powers in Paris.

The night that I was there McEnroe was scheduled for a last match against Connors, and by the time John had lost the first set it was getting quite chilly for that time of year. It was also getting late. A good crowd of two or three thousand were starting to think of home, and under the circumstances many players would have gone through the motions of another set and called it a day. But there is a flame that flickers away inside McEnroe that refuses to be snuffed out—not by a chill, damp night, or by the lateness of the hour, or by the unimportance of the occasion. For McEnroe it is important to be earnest—at the very least about the things that matter most to him.

So he kept us there another ninety minutes while he ran and fought and finally beat Connors, who doesn't like losing either. It was after 2:00 A.M. by the time we got back to the Novotel, one of those roadside chains that are scattered around France in a good plastic imitation of the American motel concept, and John was too wound up to sleep. He was also thirsty. Miraculously a young lady appeared to offer something resembling service and proceeded to squeeze fresh orange juice behind the bar while we talked.

"Thanks for keeping us up all night," I said.

He laughed and shook his head. "I don't know what it is churning away inside me, I really don't. I know exhibition matches like this offer a great opportunity to practice relaxing on court, maybe even to have a bit of fun. But I just can't let go. I still get uptight when I get a bad call. I tell myself it's no big deal, but it doesn't do any good."

McEnroe pushed his glass across the bar and produced one of the very few words in his French vocabulary. "Encore."

The girl looked at this bedraggled young man, standing there in his track suit in a deserted bar at 2:45 in the morning and replied incredulously, "You want more?" She had already squashed him enough oranges for three glasses, but she obviously wasn't familiar with an athlete's capacity for liquids after a match.

We talked some more until his thirst was quenched and the energy seeped away to be replaced by a natural state of sleepiness, and he wandered off to bed. He was still pondering the problem when he drove into the center of the city to join the other players the following

Opposite: The McEnroe overhead. *Serge Philippot*

day. Waiting on the steps of the hotel he said, "It's as if something inside me is going to burst if I don't do something to release it. It's something I haven't yet learned to control. But I reckon I'll have to find a way because I really want to take the pressure off myself and *enjoy* playing these guys."

The solution wasn't readily at hand, and a year later different problems were starting to crowd in on a young man who was beginning to find fame an increasing burden. By August 1980 he had, of course, not only won the U.S. Open but fought Borg to the death in that losing but fantastic Wimbledon final which included the unforgettable tie-breaker John simply refused to lose. Compared with the year before, he had been transformed from a promising young star into an international celebrity as far as the general public was concerned. And if anyone doesn't think that creates very special problems of its own, come and join us one evening after dinner at the Hyatt Regency Hotel in Nice. . . .

Two girls, who had been at Stanford with John, and who happened to be touring Europe that summer, were with us at a table in the corner of the bar, where a pianist was tinkling out everyone's favorite tunes. The atmosphere was mellow and relaxed. There were a couple of lovers at a nearby table, and just by the grand piano a slightly more boisterous group of middle-aged men with a couple of attractive girls were making a night of it. Later it transpired that they were the director, cast and crew of a big-budget British television commercial being made on the Côte-d'Azur.

Eventually the director, a tall, dark-haired man, with a faintly menacing expression, came over to our table and with no formal preamble butted in on our conversation. Suddenly we—and, I noticed, McEnroe in particular—were being bombarded with questions about the music, which songs we liked, etc. We all remained distantly polite and finally he meandered off.

About half an hour later, a black American who worked at a club in Cannes dropped by to say hello to the pianist and began to improvise a few songs in a deep, rich voice. The sounds were so good that we moved over to the stools around the piano.

Suddenly the director plonked himself down beside us and asked John if he knew the title of the old Cole Porter melody that we were listening to. John admitted that he didn't.

"Aren't you ashamed of yourself?" demanded the drunk, leaning across the bar belligerently. "Aren't you ashamed not to know the name of that song?"

I looked across at the girls and we all held our breath. The reaction, when it came, was much more controlled than we might have feared.

"No, I can't say I am," McEnroe replied evenly, staring down into his beer. "I don't care about your song, or you, or what you think."

"Hell, now you're getting rude," the director retorted, sniffing the scent of the brawl that he was looking for. "I reckon you've got problems, young man. What do you do anyway? I make films—so what are you good at?"

"I surf," said McEnroe. "I'm the 123rd best surfer in America."

Somehow we all managed to keep a straight face and quickly drew John back into our own conversation. The director, disappointed, returned to his party, which included a Scot in a far worse state than he was.

A little while later, having made friends with the pianist and the American singer, one of the Stanford girls agreed to sing a James Taylor number while McEnroe accompanied her, somewhat stiffly, on the piano. The director returned, tried to get one of us to admit what our friend did and then, exasperated, blurted out, "Well, I hope he plays tennis better than he plays the piano," and staggered out of the room.

But we were not done yet. It was now the Scot's turn to infiltrate the party with all the pathetic belligerence that goes hand in hand with too much whisky.

"You calling me an American—don't you dare call me an American!" he yelled at McEnroe, who hadn't called him anything. The man had already fallen off his barstool twice and broken three glasses during the course of the evening and now proceeded to collapse again. Against my better judgment I leaned down to pick him up and restored him to his uncertain pedestal, whereupon McEnroe, still incredibly unfussed by the constant baiting he had received, engaged the man in a little good-natured banter. But it was obviously going to be one of those nights when we couldn't win.

Tolerance and good humor, apparently, were not to be appreciated. A third member of the group, a striking, dark-haired girl who was presumably one of the actresses, walked up to the bar and started telling McEnroe to leave the Scottish drunk alone because he was really a very sweet, talented guy who had been working very hard and was now just a little bit tipsy. When John protested that he hadn't done anything to initiate the exchange and would be very happy to leave the guy alone if only he would let him, the girl gave him a haughty stare and said, "Oh, really, you're so conceited."

A pleasant evening had been turned into a no-win situation, and John agreed that it was time to move out. He was beginning to realize just what worldwide fame was all about. Although, thank heavens, it is highly unlikely that every bar he enters will be filled with quite such a boozy crowd as we ran into at the Hyatt, it is obvious that his reputation even then—and it hasn't got any better—set him up as a target for any loudmouthed show-off who felt the need to prove something.

That, indeed, may be the price of fame, but it is a higher price than many people might imagine. The liberties some members of the public take are barely believable. There is another instance of this kind of behavior that sticks in the memory because it was so unexpected.

Just after McEnroe and Peter Fleming had won the Benson & Hedges doubles title a couple of years ago, I was in their dressing room at Wembley. By chance John had a towel around him and Peter was dressed—they might well both have been naked—when the door was flung open by a woman in her forties with a grand but faintly Australian accent, flourishing a program.

"Here, you, sign this," she said, thrusting the program at McEnroe. "I have a young fan of yours who wants your autograph." The woman then turned to a shy girl of about twenty who was cringing in the corridor with embarrassment. When I suggested that the woman had no right to be in the players' dressing room, she gave me one of those hate-filled, unsteady stares that people can summon up when alcohol starts to take a grip of their senses.

"I've got a perfect right to ask this young man for his autograph," she replied, and then, turning back to McEnroe who was sitting, stunned and silent, in the corner, added, "Although frankly I think you are . . . Puh! That's what I think of you . . . Puh!"

By that time a tournament official had arrived, and she was escorted out, still protesting her divine right to intrude on people's privacy.

Obviously McEnroe's behavior on court and his less than charming attitude to strangers—even those who are simply trying to be nice— provoke this kind of incident. But again, contrary to what one might expect, he does not shout and scream at the interlopers and drunks. More often than not he is incredibly restrained.

After our tactical withdrawal from the Hyatt bar in Nice we all felt in need of some fresh air. So we walked across the Promenade des Anglais onto the deserted pebbled beach. The evening had still been fun, despite the interruptions, and John had put the bad parts behind him as quickly as he forgets a bad defeat. Soon he was challenging us to a contest to see how many times we could make a stone skip over the calm, warm waters of the Mediterranean. With the moon offering only a dull orange glow as it hung over Cap d'Antibes, it was difficult to follow the stones as they flipped out into the darkness, and after a while John lost interest in the challenge and bid us all good night. Happily there was no one to molest him as he shuffled back across the road into the hotel lobby, head down, hands in pockets, thinking, no doubt, that the world was a difficult and confusing sort of place.

7

LIFE AT THE TOP
IS NOT SO EASY

Even for those with the gifts of the gods and a bulging bank balance to offer proof of material rewards, life can be difficult, and complicated and a little confusing, especially when you are still very young and are being swept along on the heady wave of success, trying too hard, traveling too much and saying "yes" to too many people. All that McEnroe discovered the hard way in the first months of 1980 as injury hit, form slipped and criticism mounted.

The first disappointment was the loss of his Masters crown. Ironically it was friend and neighbor Vitas Gerulaitis who paved the way for his downfall at Madison Square Garden. Along with Borg, Vilas and all the other top point winners of the year-long Grand Prix tour of 1979, Gerulaitis had elected to play in the New York showpiece this time, and after successfully negotiating the early round-robin matches, the pair met on Friday night to decide who would finish on top of his group. The $10,000 bonus for finishing as a group winner was the lesser of two incentives, the greater being the fact that the winner would meet Connors in the knockout semifinal while the loser would have to face Borg.

Maybe after his loss in the final of the U.S. Open four months earlier, Gerulaitis had more to prove. Maybe he had a fraction more incentive to drive himself on, not so much toward victory, but away from the haunting specter of another defeat at the hands of his New York rival. Not that McEnroe was exactly giving anything away, but one sensed that the greater motivation was surging from Gerulaitis' side of the net. But motivation itself is never enough. On this particular night Vitas had the tools to finish the job—a much steadier and more penetrating serve, an instinctive knowledge of his opponent's game that only heightened his already electric speed about court, and increasing confidence on the return of serve which blunted one of McEnroe's most potent weapons. It was enough, although the 3–6, 7–6, 7–6 score revealed just how close it was.

So McEnroe's opponent in the semifinal was to be Borg. And again he was up against a man with a special sense of motivation—as if playing the American left-hander wasn't motivation enough for this proud Swede. But this time there was something else, because Björn was well aware of what everybody had been saying, and it irked him. They were saying, after his defeats at the U.S. Open, that he couldn't win in New York. And New York, especially Madison Square Garden, was the place where the greatest champions in sport were expected to put their talent and their courage on the line and, if they were truly champions, emerge triumphant. In addition, Borg had never won the Masters, even when it was a nomadic event, moving from city to city around the world. So he wanted this one badly.

For a time it didn't look as if McEnroe would let him have it. Using his incredible touch to jerk the Swede around court, John fought back from 2–4 in the first set to win it on the tie-break. Borg was still having trouble with his timing midway through the second until, at 4–3, a typical backhand pass left the New Yorker groping in its wake, and the all-important breach was made. Winning the set 6–3, Borg still couldn't break free until he raised his game to a new plateau of excellence in the deciding tie-break and took advantage of a surprisingly wild, slashing forehand volley from his rival on the fifth point to wrap it up by the unexpectedly lopsided margin of 7 points to 1.

Borg hushed the New York crowd into awestruck silence by beating Gerulaitis for the fifteenth consecutive time in the final. The score was 6–2, 6–2, and the game took just 76 minutes. So Björn Borg, to his obvious delight, was the new Master and still the No. 1 player in the world. McEnroe had work to do.

For a player who had been winning virtually at will in the latter months of 1979, the work load suddenly seemed to get heavier. Inexperience was the root of the problem. Thinking match play alone would keep him fit, McEnroe filled his schedule with too many tournaments and never gave his body a chance to recover from minor aches and strains. And, of course, he was never very good at doing the preventive exercise that even a body about to enter its twenty-first year requires to keep it properly tuned.

So the defeats began to pile up. A wounding five-set loss to Connors in the final of the U.S. Pro Indoors in Philadelphia, after he had been on court at the Spectrum most of the previous day in singles and doubles, was the next setback. The effort left him emotionally as well as physically drained, for, as Laurie Pignon observed in the London *Daily Mail,* the crowd behaved like a mob. "The match had all the atmosphere of a street fight," wrote Pignon. "The crowd clapped McEnroe's ten double faults and they clapped when he fell over three times." The pressure of always being the villain of the piece was beginning to tell.

He gained some measure of revenge by beating Connors 7–6, 7–6 in the final of the U.S. National Indoors at Memphis, and there were title-winning triumphs, too, in WCT tournaments in Richmond, Virginia, and Milan during the first three months of the year. But he went down to Gerulaitis again in the Pepsi Grand Slam in Florida; was forced to pull out of WCT Frankfurt through injury; lost his way on the red clay of the Monte Carlo Country Club against Vilas; and was beaten 6–4, 6–1 by Harold Solomon in the quarterfinal of the Alan King Classic in Las Vegas. But most demoralizing of all, perhaps, was the thumping defeat that the United States suffered at the hands of Argentina and the raucously partisan Buenos Aires crowd in the Davis Cup. McEnroe was beaten by both Vilas and Clerc after not having conceded so much as a set in eleven previous Davis Cup singles.

So it was a slightly chastened young man who arrived in Dallas to defend his WCT crown, but a realistic one. "In the long run the Buenos Aires experience probably did me good. I've had a few problems, sure, but to give yourself excuses is the wrong approach."

Again one marveled at the inner strength and outward maturity of this youngster who was already laboring under the nickname of "Super Brat." He continued to take his beatings like a man, even though there was no immediate improvement in his form. The irrepressible Connors snatched away his WCT title in a four-set Dallas final; and a week later, having battled his way through to the final of the WCT Tournament of Champions on clay at Forest Hills, Gerulaitis got him again—6–0 in the third.

After that the prospect of the French Open and the even slower clay at Stade Roland Garros was daunting in the extreme, and McEnroe never looked remotely capable of living up to the No. 2 seeding he had earned solely on the basis of his ATP computer ranking. "One year I am going to prepare properly for the French," he told me, for neither the first nor the last time. Even though he managed to win love sets against a veteran clay-courter, Patrice Dominguez, in the first round and a younger one, Per Hjertquist, in the second, he was never quite sure enough of his own ability to stem the brilliantly sustained attack he met from the bobbing, weaving, bouncing Australian Paul McNamee and lost a wildly exciting and spectacular dogfight 7–6, 6–7, 7–6, 7–6.

So it was hardly surprising that McEnroe was relieved to see the grass at the Queen's Club when he arrived in England in June for what he had promised himself would be a carefully planned assault on Wimbledon. After making a mess of it for two years in a row, he knew that he could not afford any more bad losses in the world's premier tournament if he was to be recognized as a valid contender for the crown Borg had been wearing with such style for the previous four years.

Even though the first of the really vicious press criticism had hit him during the Stella Artois Championships at Queen's the year before, he had come to enjoy the tournament. The reasons were very simple. Both tournament director Clive Bernstein and advertising wizard Frank Lowe, whose company has been responsible for all those wonderful caricatures of Nastase, Connors and McEnroe that are plastered on billboards all over London prior to the event each year, had gone out of their way to be nice to him and make him feel at home. Quite naturally he responded, and by the time he made his third consecutive appearance in the championships, Bernstein was publicly calling him "a true professional who never lets the public down."

That made a welcome change to some of the things that had been written about him the previous year after a series of minor incidents blew up into a raging inferno of a row during a quarterfinal match against Sandy Mayer. Sandy, who has not always been the most civil of players himself, fanned the flames by suggesting McEnroe should be banned, and the press took it from there. "Go Home, Super Brat!" screamed the tabloids, picking up on a phrase penned by Ian Barnes of the London *Daily Express* in a slightly different context a few months earlier.

But soon it wasn't just the headlines that made McEnroe shake his head in wonderment and disbelief. In the *Daily Express,* ace feature writer Jean Rook was sharpening her quill, and when she jabs that weapon, it hurts. While admitting that John was quite nice to her when they met, she announced people said he was "loud, rude, vain, childish, sulky and bloody-minded. John McEnroe, at twenty, is a spoilt child only his mother could love." That little homily was spread across nine columns of the paper. And there were others like it. Apart from being hurt, McEnroe was genuinely perplexed.

"I mean, I know I lost my cool and shouted at a couple of people when I shouldn't have, but I didn't expect everyone to react like they did. I thought they might understand or give me a second chance or forgive or whatever. I couldn't believe it was blown up into such a big deal."

But now he was back in a calmer frame of mind. As is often the case, a little adversity had done him good. The third-round loss to McNamee in Paris had given him a few days off and the chance to settle into the flat that he and Stacy were renting for the month he expected to be in London. That, hopefully, would eliminate the popping flashbulbs that had greeted him every time he stepped out of the Kensington Hilton during the previous year's Wimbledon.

Following the wonderful caricatures of Nastase and Connors, McEnroe's mop-top became the symbol of the huge billboard advertising that Frank Lowe's agency used to publicize the Stella Artois Championships at the Queen's Club in London.

"I'm so relaxed I can hardly believe it myself," he told John Oakley of the *Evening News.* "I'm not saying I'll never blow my top again or start screaming at umpires, but I honestly don't want it. I want the British public to see there is another side of John McEnroe, that I am not just the big bullyboy they all believe I am."

He certainly got off to a good start. No sooner had Queen's started in typical monsoon conditions that Laurie Pignon was suggesting he deserved a medal for agreeing to play the big-serving Californian Tom Leonard "with a suspect ankle, on an outside court made dangerous by rain." But he did it because Bernstein asked him to, and he was leading 6–3, 3–4 when the referee decided conditions were simply too bad to continue. He won soon enough when play resumed and went on to beat Australia's Kim Warwick in the final after eliminating in the semis the man he had beaten in the 1979 final, Paraguay's languid, talented giant Victor Pecci.

So, despite the risks he had taken playing on wet grass, the ankle, heavily strapped, had come through unscathed and was growing stronger day by day. Despite the rain and the frustrations of trying to find a practice court, his own weather chart seemed set fair. The omens were correct. Three weeks later the tennis world was in a state of euphoria after what many described as the greatest Wimbledon final of all time. Borg had done it again, but this time McEnroe was also the hero after a match that was nothing less than a celebration of the modern game. More than the excitement, I recall it now as a joyous occasion for all of us who love tennis. I tried to capture that mood in the report I wrote for *Tennis Week:*

After two of the wettest and most frustrating weeks in the history of the Championships, it came as such sweet thunder—this final of finals, this clash of titans, gracing the world's most famous sporting stage as it had never been graced before.

Twice, as Björn Borg climbed still higher on his endless ladder to the stars, the sun peeped out and, then, as if in shame, disappeared again behind the familiar blanket of cloud. Begone fickle friend! We did not need you to illuminate this glorious scene.

Two men of skill and steel, locking their talents and courage in a battle so closely fought that only the genius of the game's scoring system could divide them, needed no assistance nor, heaven forbid, any further disturbance from the elements. They had ploughed through rain and hail; skidded on slippery grass and dug deep into muddy base-lines on their way to this great finale and, once there, it was they who produced the thunder and the lightning, sending shock-waves of electricity through the enraptured Centre Court.

All they needed was a stage to play their game. And what a game they played! Was there ever a better final than this? Has one match ever produced dramas, tenacity, power and sportsmanship in greater abundance? Can anyone now deny that Björn Borg is one of the greatest players of all time or that John McEnroe stands on the very threshold of greatness?

While we ponder these questions, let us savour the memory of this remarkable contest for we shall be fortunate indeed to see its like again. Borg and McEnroe will doubtless play many more great matches—already they have produced three other classic encounters at Richmond, New Orleans and in the Masters last January—but it will take a great many factors and no little luck for them to arrive in the Wimbledon final a second time and play as well again.

We are getting spoiled with our finals at Wimbledon. Unlike the previous two decades when a Trabert, a Hoad, or a Laver would frequently crush some hapless opponent, the seventies provided a plethora of excitement on finals day. Smith-Nastase; Ashe-Connors; the first Borg-Connors; and last year's Borg-Tanner were all great matches and now this, which may be the greatest of all.

For once the statistics alone reveal something of the drama. Björn Borg became Wimbledon Champion for the fifth successive year by defeating John McEnroe 1–6, 7–5, 6–3, 6–7, 8–6 with the fourth-set tie-break stretching to 18 points to 16. McEnroe eventually won that set on his seventh set-point and Borg finally won the match on his eighth match-point. And if further evidence is needed of just how close this 3-hour 53-minute marathon really was, the total number of points and games won and lost will do it. Borg won 190 points to McEnroe's 186 and 28 games to his opponent's 27.

At the beginning Borg was surprisingly bad. The mistakes that spun off his racket were partially due to the wicked accuracy of McEnroe's shots and partially as a result of his failure to anticipate just how much faster the worn, brown Centre Court had become after a couple of days' respite from the rain. The racket he began with was, by his own very special standards, too loose, and when McEnroe had served to love for a 3–0 lead, Borg changed it for a tighter one.

But it was not until the eleventh game of the second set, when he held serve to love, having settled on the tactics of coming in behind his first serve and staying back on his second, that he could finally look McEnroe in the eye with any degree of confidence. By that time he had escaped from four break-points; three of them in the crucial ninth game. The Swede had opened that game with his fourth double fault but on each of the three occasions that McEnroe stood within a point of a 5–4 lead with his serve to follow, Borg greeted the crisis with a vicious first serve. As the drama unfolded, the value and importance of those three magnificent deliveries grew. A two set to love deficit might well have been too big a gap to bridge against McEnroe in this mood—even for Borg.

So, at 5–6, McEnroe served to save the set and suddenly gave Borg a foot in the door by dumping one intended stop volley into the net and then foolishly attempting another off the very next point. McEnroe's exquisite touch is sometimes good enough to outwit Borg, but the timing has to be perfect and this time it was not. Björn raced on to it and tapped away a winner, 15–30. Then came the killer blow. Lunging into his left, Borg hammered a superb double-fisted backhand down the line off precisely the kind of first serve that was supposed to be McEnroe's most potent weapon.

It gave Borg two set-points and he clinched it on the second when McEnroe netted a backhand volley off another fine service return.

More fine service returns helped Borg to an early lead in the third but he had to fight his way out of a 0–40 situation in the seventh game before serving out for 6–3. By this stage, it was becoming a duel of the highest class. Both men had honed their game to near perfection, sprinkling the wrinkled court with power and guile and so much skill that even the bad bounces were handled with a deft turn of the wrist or adjustment of the racket head.

At 4–4 in the magnificent fourth set, Borg forced another breach in the New Yorker's armour. Again it was his ability to meet McEnroe's sizzling first serve, which flew at him off the apex of the service box, with a crushing cross-court return that earned him the break, and when he reached double match-point at 40–15 in the next game, we prepared for the end.

It was then that the twenty-one-year-old American wrote himself into the folklore of the game, proving, for those who still doubted it, that his strength of character matched his skill. The few fools who had booed him when he walked on court for his first Wimbledon final might have hurt his pride but they strengthened his resolve, not merely to play his best tennis but to prove he could put that combustible temperament under lock and key and treat triumph and disaster with the equanimity of a man called Borg. This he did throughout the match and when he hit Björn with a firm backhand pass down the line on the first match-point and a forehand pass on the second, the crowd realized the Swede was not the only player out there with nerves of steel.

A great backhand service return sealed the break back and soon we were into the historic tie-break—surely the most dramatic ever played in a major championship final. It stretched over 22 minutes and 34 points—more than would be needed to win an entire set 6–1—and was so finely balanced that match-points and set-points seemed to ricochet back and forth across the court with the blur of syncopated rhythm. If there were unforced errors, they were lost and forgotten amidst the music of balls exploding off gut as these two maestros struck chords of power and precision.

One remembers Borg rifling a backhand pass down the line to reach match-point at 6–5; a featherweight drop volley from McEnroe at one moment and then, facing another match-point, a lifesaving lunge to smack home another volley with the speed of hand and eye that would have made a panther blink. In between the even points, the sequence built crisis by crisis with Borg reaching two match-points (his third and fourth of the match) at 6–5 and 7–6; then McEnroe with two set-points; then Borg back on the threshold again with three more match-points and then a run of four set-points for the American before he clinched it on the fifth with a heavily top-spun service return that was dipping too quickly for Borg to control as he tried for an ambitious stop volley.

The Centre Court erupted. John McEnroe Senior was out of his seat and Junior was clenching his fists and staring at the heavens. Two sets all; seven match-points dead and buried and the match vibrating with life. The greatest title in tennis was still up for grabs. Could the implacable Swede—the Centre Court's immovable object for the past four years—hold onto his treasured crown? Once again the answer was yes.

Borg did it by thrusting the disappointment of those lost match-points from his mind—it took him, as he admitted afterwards, a couple of games to do so—and launched himself into as fine a bout of sustained serving as I have ever seen in a fifth set of a Championship match. None of the great servers in Wimbledon's history has surpassed it—not Newcombe, not Smith, not Tanner not even Hoad.

Eighty percent of his first serves found their mark. Incredibly McEnroe could win only three points against serve in the entire set and it was a tribute to his own resilience and skill that the young New Yorker stayed with the Champion for as long as he did. Twice he served confidently to save the match but in the fourteenth game, Borg unleashed two superb returns and reached his eighth match-point when John netted a low volley. This time

Opposite: The McEnroe serve. *Tony Duffy*

it really was the end. One more deadly backhand cross-court pass and that was it.

"I am as constant as the northern star," Caesar said before Brutus and his conspirators proved him wrong. But McEnroe was alone out there and, well as he wielded it, one dagger was not enough to fell this Caesar.

This Nordic Emperor is as constant a factor as the game has ever known and he is not done yet. In fact his powers are growing still. Thank God for McEnroe for otherwise Borg would indeed "bestride this narrow world and hold the palm alone."

McEnroe's path to the final had been uneven. He had been dreading a return to the notorious No. 2 Court, that graveyard of dreams where he, like many aspiring champions before him, had lost so unexpectedly to Tim Gullikson twelve months before. But in fact this time it was on the adjoining No. 3 Court that he had been given his biggest scare. Playing with the carefree abandon of a man on the verge of giving up the game, Terry Rocavert, a lowly ranked Australian, led McEnroe by two sets to one before going down 6–3 in the fifth. Tom Okker, Kevin Curren (a powerful young South African who pushed him to 7–5, 7–6, 7–6) and none other than Peter Fleming were the next hurdles he cleared successfully, not merely from the point of view of the result but also because the volatile temper was kept largely in check.

But the semifinal was a different matter. The semifinal meant Jimmy Connors. It also presented the psychological barrier of being the stage of the Championship he had never managed to pass before. As far as the state of his nerves was concerned, it was a tougher match for him than facing Borg in the final. He couldn't afford to lose to Jimmy again so soon after Dallas—not if he wanted to retain the No. 2 ranking his U.S. Open victory had secured for him.

So, although the match, once it got under way, was rarely in doubt despite a courageous fight back by Connors which earned him the second set, McEnroe was too tense to control his temper when a few decisions went against him. Once the umpire refused to award him an ace after a fault had been wrongly signaled. The umpire wanted to play two. "If in your opinion, my opponent could not have reached the ball, it should be my point," said McEnroe angrily. But despite the fact that he was right and despite the fact that he didn't swear and actually remembered to say "please" at the start of the conversation, the crowd immediately started whistling and slow handclapping. Tanner had also made a similar complaint during his match with Connors in the previous round. But Tanner comes across as the clean-cut all-American boy and no one whistles at him. They whistle at McEnroe not because he is wrong, not because he swears, but just because of his reputation and the way he looks. His behavior had been virtually impeccable for the

The end of the great struggle between Borg and McEnroe for the Wimbledon title in 1980. While Borg kisses the cup, McEnroe watches from the sidelines—but for how long? *Serge Philippot*

previous ten days, but one angry outburst was enough. It is small wonder that, as time has passed, he has occasionally felt the effort of trying to behave well just simply isn't worth it. "So many times the crowd never understands what I am trying to say and just never gives me a chance," he complains. "I have a perfect right to point out to an umpire politely that he has made an error."

But, of course, as the umpire gives him the stony stare and the crowd gives him the whistle, the resentment and frustration build to a point where a rational complaint turns into a raging torrent of abuse. It never got to that level of intensity against Connors, thank goodness, and with another masterly performance McEnroe was through to a final that would do more for his reputation and self-esteem than any other he has played so far.

However, his year of highs and lows continued. He lost to Jose-Luis Clerc, the rapidly improving young Argentinian, for the second time in six months in the final of the Grand Prix event at South Orange, New Jersey; was forced to scratch through injury during his second-round match against Erik Van Dillen in the Canadian Open; and then, in one of the few times he has ever gone out in the first round, crashed 7–6, 6–4 to Tracy Austin's brother, John, in Atlanta. Hardly the best preparation for the defense of his U.S. Open crown the following week.

But once again McEnroe rose to the big occasion and proved that, like his arch-rival Borg, he too is a proud and brilliant guardian of a hard-earned crown. Ivan Lendl, who was starting to look very threatening indeed, pushed him to 7–5 in the fourth set of a rugged quarterfinal clash, and then he found Connors—who else?—waiting for him in the semis. The most interesting aspect of this latest encounter was the fact that the defending champion was able to blow his cool over a series of dubious line-calls, totally to lose his rhythm and concentration, to allow Connors to run off a string of eleven consecutive games and still come back to win 6–4, 5–7, 0–6, 6–3, 7–6. McEnroe won the deciding tie-break comfortably enough by 7 points to 3, but Connors had played to the very limit of his considerable ability; and quite apart from McEnroe's tantrums, the match exuded a cutthroat quality between these two less than friendly rivals that only heightened the sense of drama. It was a match made for New York, and its pitch of excitement almost made one forget the roar of the 727 engines as the jets climbed off the end of the La Guardia Airport runway.

But, as at Wimbledon, a match with Connors seemed to drain McEnroe of all the worst excesses of his combustible temperament and leave him primed and coolly determined for the task of playing Borg.

After that great triumph at Wimbledon, this seemed to be Borg's best ever opportunity of nailing down the one major title that still eluded him. But after coming back from the dead three times in as many rounds—two sets to one down against Tanner in the quarters; two sets to love down against the mercurial little South African, Johan Kriek, in the semis; and two sets to love down against McEnroe in the final—Björn's quest for the Grand Slam died where he least expected it, in the fifth set.

On fourteen occasions since 1976 Borg had been extended to a fifth set by a variety of worthy challengers in various tournaments, but always he had proved himself the calmer, tougher competitor when the chips were down. But not this time, not under lights on a cool September evening at Flushing Meadow, not against John McEnroe. This time, in a mighty test of stamina and skill, it was the New York left-hander who wrenched the prize of victory from the game's most bemedaled warrior. The score by which McEnroe retained his crown was 7–6, 6–1, 6–7, 5–7, 6–4. It contained the same number of games, 55, as their vintage Wimbledon final and, at 4 hours 13 minutes, lasted 20 minutes longer.

It was a strange match: strange for the way in which Borg squandered his chances when he twice served for the first set; strange for the way he slumped into a fit of near-suicidal depression in the second; and strange for the way he fought back only to lose momentum in the home stretch he knows so well. But apparently his astrological chart was a mess that week, so maybe it was all in the stars. But McEnroe, the Aquarian, was only interested in keeping body and mind together in a last Herculean bid to save his crown. He was into his ninth hour of singles play in twenty-four hours.

"In the fourth set I thought my body was falling apart," McEnroe admitted. "But then I felt better; better, in fact, in the fifth set than I had done at Wimbledon."

God alone knows how. If his body didn't actually fall apart on him, it virtually refused to function the day following the final. "I couldn't get out of bed, man. I tell you, my body just packed up." No wonder. But when the will to win is as strong as it is in this amazing young man, adrenaline will keep a body pumping past the point of exhaustion, and it was that kind of will that Borg had to face in the fifth set. And for once it proved stronger than his own.

Aided by two Borg double faults, McEnroe seized control of that deciding set by snatching a 4–3 lead and then unleashed a series of superb serves, dropping only two points on his remaining two service games. To the amazement of many, McEnroe had proved himself the greater champion on the day, but with Borg still champion of Wimbledon and France, John knew better than to start proclaiming himself No. 1 in the world. Impatient on court, he remained almost Job-like in his patience off it, but he knew now, deep down inside his private self, that it was only a matter of time. It was Wimbledon that mattered most. He needed Wimbledon.

Even though it is easy to look back now and realize that his defeat at Flushing Meadow in 1980 tolled a bell of distant doom in the glorious career of Björn Borg, I said at the time that, by the infinitesimal standards by which we judge great champions, he would never again be quite the same player. I knew he would continue to win big titles occasionally, and as long as his enthusiasm lasted, he would continue to play great tennis. But suddenly he was no longer invulnerable at those moments that separate the quick from the dead. A doubt had been implanted in a previously undoubting mind. And McEnroe would never let him forget it.

8

A MESSY MASTERS—
AND RAPID REAPPRAISAL

Whatever seeds of doubt McEnroe had managed to implant in Borg's subconscious, the results were far from instantaneous. When I met McEnroe for a prearranged interview that I had been asked to do for an American magazine, it was his face that seemed to be etched with anxiety about the final outcome of their encounter. We were back at Madison Square Garden for the 1981 Volvo Masters. I found him on the trainer's bench being attended to by one of the great characters of the pro tour, the John Denver look-alike, Bill Norris. For a man who spends much of his life cooped up in windowless rooms tending to athlete's limbs, Bill retains a weird and wonderfully inventive sense of humor. He is also exceptionally good at his job.

With McEnroe in the state I found him that afternoon, Bill had a special task on his hands. "You could say my condition's not too good, that's for sure," John volunteered. One could tell that just by looking at him. For a start he was overweight; he also had a stomach problem, brought on partially by excess tension, and he had strained his thigh.

"Actually it was a pulled hamstring," I was informed later by Dave Fechtman, the lanky Texan who is the ATP's other trainer on the tour and, with degrees in science, biology and physical education from North Texas State University, is, like Norris, highly qualified for his specialized profession. "Between the ages of nineteen and twenty-five there is still a significant degree of bone growth and stabilization going on in the human body," Fechtman explained. "And playing tennis at this level on an almost constant basis subjects the body to a tremendous amount of stress. But John handles it pretty well. More than some players he is prepared to play with a minor injury and endure a certain amount of pain as result. Like Connors, I would say he is exceptional in that respect."

There was little doubt that McEnroe had been playing in pain at the Garden, but as usual he wasn't trotting out any excuses in press conferences. He didn't really need to after his Thursday night duel with Borg, which had turned out to be another little classic, if not for the standard of play, then at least for the drama extracted from a score of 6–4, 6–7, 7–6. Pouncing on errors from an erratic opponent, the Swede won the final tie-break by 7 points to 2, but he did something else during the course of the match that will be remembered much longer. He argued with the umpire. The crowd of nineteen thousand sat aghast as the master walked up to British umpire Mike Lugg and complained about a call. But even when Lugg told him he was overruling the baseline judge on the call, Björn went on complaining—very quietly. Eventually Lugg was forced to become the first umpire ever to dock Borg, first one, and then a second penalty point for refusing to play. Björn was very stubborn, and very angry, too.

"I was in total shock," McEnroe told the press. "I mean, I didn't believe what I was seeing. I didn't know whether to tank the next two points, to make up for the points Björn had lost, or what. I certainly didn't want to take the set that way, because, of course, the penalties gave me set points in the tie-break at 6–3. I just didn't feel right about it."

For different reasons he didn't feel very right about his match with Gene Mayer either, and when he lost to the double-handed player from New Jersey for the first time in his career, he had effectively blown his chances of qualifying for the semifinals. But there was still the doubles to play for, and he wasn't about to let Peter Fleming down just because of a sore leg. (They went on to win the doubles title with a straight-set victory over the year's entertaining WCT Braniff champions, Peter McNamara and Paul McNamee.)

So McEnroe was on the bench being patched up when I started questioning him about a whole range of subjects, beginning with his attitude toward keeping himself in shape.

"It's not good, is it?" he smiled. "I suppose I don't do enough exercise. I'm definitely not the most enthusiastic trainer in the world. I prefer just to play a lot to keep myself fit. But I am beginning to realize that is not enough. Arthur Ashe has recommended a gym here in New York and it's probably about time I did something about it."

Although the gym never got to see very much of him, McEnroe certainly did something about his physical condition, because within a matter of weeks he had lost a startling amount of weight, mostly as a result of a proper diet that cut out a lot of the junk food of which he was so fond. What had probably been lingering puppy fat disappeared, and he never looked the same again.

He also started talking about the problems of being a star and how difficult he found it being a worldwide celebrity.

"I don't really consider myself a celebrity," he declared. "I don't like

A crowd of nineteen thousand stare in disbelief as Björn Borg argues with British umpire Mike Lugg during the Volvo Masters at Madison Square Garden in 1981, and eventually gets docked two penalty points. Borg was playing John McEnroe wh was, perhaps, more amazed than anyone. *Serge Philippot*

what goes with it. I want to be myself. I want to be known as a top tennis player but not all the other bullshit that goes with it. I don't like being a phony, and that's what happens when you start meeting hundreds of different people all over the place. I prefer to be honest. I think that's more important than being liked by everyone. But I know I have to learn to handle people, and you could say there's still some room for improvement there!"

The U.S. boycott of the Moscow Olympics had been the hot topic of the preceding months, but McEnroe had no wish to air his views for public record: "I'd love to talk about that subject for hours but, really who cares what I think? Politics should be left to politicians. I don't know all the facts. Even Ronald Reagan didn't know everything that was going on in the White House when he was running for President. I'd like to see athletes do well because I'm an athlete. But I've never been to Russia. I don't know what's going on. I think it's totally inappropriate for someone to sound off about something just because he's in the limelight. He's no different from anyone else and certainly no more important when it comes to politics. There are probably a lot of union workers in New Jersey who know a hell of a lot more about politics than I do. But, privately, I like to keep abreast of events. I think it's important to be informed."

I wondered as he finished that little speech how many other supposedly spoiled twenty-one-year-old superstars had such a rational, modest and intelligent understanding of their place in the world.

We went on to discuss a decision he had come to a few weeks earlier that did have political connotations—an invitation that he and Borg had received to play an exhibition match in the black South African state of Bophuthatswana. Borg had been ready to go despite heavy criticism in the Swedish press, but McEnroe, who had been guaranteed a staggering $800,000 for one afternoon's work, had turned it down. I asked him why:

"Well, after discussing it with my father and listening to the opinions of a few people who knew something about the situation down there, we both agreed that there was an element of exploitation in the whole thing.

"I just didn't like the idea of being used to show off a supposedly black state that appears to exist at the convenience of the South African government. I don't want to get into details because, as I have said, I don't believe in coming out with heavy statements about things that I don't know much about. And as I've never been to South Africa and have no particular desire to go there, I obviously can't comment with any degree of accuracy. It was just a feeling I had; call it instinct if you like.

"And in any case, I'm not sure these types of challenge matches are particularly good for the game. It depends on the time and the place. It's possible that Borg and I will do a tour of Australia, although the money will be a lot less than we were offered from South Africa. But that's Australia, which is a bit different."

In fact, McEnroe and Borg did play a three-match series in Australia the following month before John was properly fit. He lost badly in the first two matches and was humbly apologetic to the Australian press. "I feel embarrassed," he told them. "You don't want people to think badly of all this because of all the money involved. All I can do is play my guts out and try to salvage something in the last match in Melbourne." He did, and won. The money that the pair were guaranteed was fractionally more than half what they would have received in South Africa. The original date for the South African match, December 6, 1980, was left free on McEnroe's calendar, so he flew down to Florida to play an exhibition for Harold Solomon's Hunger Project Charity. Instead of $800,000, he received nothing.

In light of all this, his reply to my next question was rather sad, despite being truthful for quite different reasons. I asked him if he could change one thing about himself, what it would be:

"My image. I know I don't help myself by arguing with umpires and answering back when the spectators start yelling abuse at me. I know that's stupid because you can't win. But I just hope that one day they'll understand what I'm trying to say—that it's wrong in tennis to applaud double faults, or scream out when you are about to serve, or do any of those dumb things a few spectators do. That's probably too much to hope, and I'm not sure how long it will take me to change. I'll probably go right out there now and get into an argument with someone. I just can't help myself. I really can't. If I see something that's wrong, I just have to say so. You could say I have a temper. I'm Irish, you know."

That winsome, impish and somehow shy smile crossed his face and I wished, not for the first time, that he could carry it on court with him. It would prove so much more effective a weapon in righting the wrongs that pain him than that belligerent scowl. But as long as he feels the way he does, replacing the scowl with a smile would require wearing a mask, and that he simply cannot do. To John McEnroe, so logical, rational and intelligent in so many ways, that would amount to being a phony. He knows it would probably help him. He knows it would probably achieve more than he is achieving now. But deep, deep down in the very fiber of his proud and stubborn being, there is something that keeps telling him that there is nothing worse in the world than pretending to be something you are not.

So he heaved his body off the table, changed for his doubles with

Peter Fleming and went out to face the music. About half an hour later, as I was typing in the press room, I heard the boos and I knew that he was at it again, scowling at the world, creating his own special kind of misery. As usual he had left his smile, folded with his sneakers and jeans, back in the locker room.

Once the weight came off and the hamstring mended, McEnroe's fortunes began to pick up again on the WCT tour in Europe. He won tournaments in Milan and Frankfurt; and then returned to Dallas to scythe his way through a Borg-less field to regain the crown he had lost the year before by beating Johan Kriek in the final.

But even with a flat in Montmartre, five days' peaceful practice and Stacy to keep him company, the French Open still turned out to be another struggle through quicksand. On courts made soggy by a depressingly wet Parisian spring, he beat Vince Van Patten in the first round and then actually managed to get past three South American clay-courters—former ATP president Jaime Fillol, Uruguay's Diego Perez, and an old rival from his junior days, Ricardo Ycaza of Ecuador—to reach the quarterfinals. That, by his own limited standards in Paris—winning the mixed with Mary Carillo in 1977 was still by far his best achievement there—was some kind of progress, but the fact that the unknown Perez, a qualifier, had taken him to four sets did not augur well for his ability to handle sterner opposition. And sterner stuff was indeed just around the corner.

Ivan Lendl had never beaten McEnroe before, but the twenty-one-year-old Czech had already stamped his mark on the tennis world by leading his country to victory in the Davis Cup, having achieved, in the semifinals of the 1980 competition, the remarkable feat of beating both Vilas and Clerc in Buenos Aires. Clay was his surface and he knew that, at last, he had got McEnroe where he wanted him. By the time McEnroe had finally persuaded referee Jacques Dorfmann to halt play for the night after loud complaints about the wet and gloomy conditions, Lendl's pounding ground strokes had caught the American out of position on a sufficient number of occasions to secure a 6–4, 6–4, 0–3 lead. On the resumption, McEnroe managed to cling to his service break to lead 5–3, but then everything came apart at the seams and Lendl bludgeoned his way to victory, 7–5, for a thoroughly convincing straight-set win.

I asked McEnroe what he thought about his performance:

"Well, I'd say disgraceful is just about the best way of putting it. Conditions were just a little different today and I adjusted slower than he did. The ball was coming through harder and I just wasn't ready for it. I was making careless mistakes. I'm unhappy because I feel I didn't

The power and athleticism of Ivan Lendl—in action here at the U.S. Open at Flushing Meadow—threaten McEnroe's position as the No. 1 player in the world. *Serge Philippot*

play the way I know I could have. I'm not hitting the ball the way I should. Everything's wrong. It's my fault, no one else's. There's no reason why I shouldn't be able to play on clay, so it must be a question of preparation or mental toughness or something."

Another honest appraisal. As he says, there is no reason technically why he should not be able to win the French Open. Serve-and-volley players like Roy Emerson and Fred Stolle with less all-round equipment than McEnroe have done it. One day he will, too. But in Paris in 1981 he achieved little other than to give Ivan Lendl, who eventually lost to Borg in the final, a foot in the door in their increasingly antagonistic personal rivalry. It proved to be a psychological boost that the Czech was to exploit to the full later in the year.

9
WIMBLEDON 1981

Once again the 1981 Stella Artois Championship at the Queen's Club at the beginning of June offered a little preview of what was to come for John McEnroe. There was a bad-tempered confrontation with the big Californian Hank Pfister and unnecessary baiting of umpire Georgina Clark during his defeat of Brian Gottfried in the final. With Wimbledon looming—a Wimbledon he was now certain he could win—McEnroe was feeling the pressure.

His premonitions were quite correct but his preparation, at least on the emotional level, was all wrong. By the time he stepped on No. 1 Court for his first-round match against Tom Gullikson, the left-handed twin, he was so nervous and strung so taut that the inevitable happened. As he admitted candidly some time later:

"I lost control of myself. I probably didn't realize it was as bad as it looked. I didn't feel I had done anything that terrible by the time I got the second warning. But there were all sorts of things building up inside that I couldn't control. Everything aggravated me because I had put so much pressure on myself to do well. Even before the match started, the umpire came up to me as I was sitting on court and said, 'I'm Scottish—so we're not going to have any problems now are we?' I suppose he was trying to break the ice and make out we would understand each other because I am Irish or something. But when I didn't respond, he got visibly annoyed. So that was a bad beginning right there. But I just don't want to have any personal contact with officials. I just find the whole thing too difficult. It's business out there and there is no room for personal relationships."

Most of the business in that match wasn't very pleasant. Although he won handily enough, 7–6, 7–5, 6–3, he was so uncertain of himself that he was continually mocking his own efforts; and in one outburst that would have been funny if all the other stuff hadn't been going on, he announced to the crowd, "I'm so disgusting you shouldn't watch. Everybody leave!"

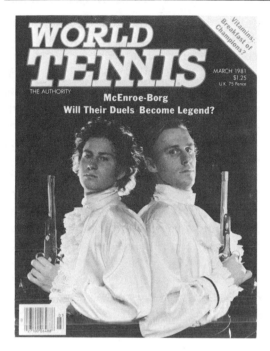

World Tennis' image of the
duel that was building up
between McEnroe and Borg
for the coveted Wimbledon title.
Copyright CBS, Inc., 1981

Sadly, of course, it was his attitude toward the officials that most people found disgusting—not his tennis. He was rude to the Scottish umpire Edward James, yelled at linesmen, insulted the referee when Fred Hoyles appeared to try to restore order, smashed his racket and then refused to shake hands with the umpire at the end. The crowd booed him off court, but even as he went, a young girl flung her arms around his neck and said, "I love you."

Maybe, just maybe, she was one of the few to see through the scowling, pouting, petulant visage and catch a glimpse of the insecurities that lay beneath. But no one had much time for thoughts like those. Super Brat was back with a vengeance as far as the press was concerned, and all the good work of the previous year's final had been torn to shreds. The headlines screamed for his blood and completely dwarfed his remarks afterward, which, as usual, were contrite, self-searching and honest. "My behavior is unnecessary," he said. "I'm the one who gets hurt. No one is to blame but myself. If other players manage to keep calm, why not me?"

The question was left hanging as McEnroe progressed steadily through the championships, but for many, different questions were more pertinent. If he had been so bad, why hadn't he been defaulted? The answer lay somewhere in the complicated penalty structure as laid down in the Grand Prix Code of Conduct—since revised—and the reluctance of Fred Hoyles to take such drastic action. As it was, McEnroe got hit with a $1,500 fine for the Gullikson match and was warned that any further misconduct would be interpreted as "aggravated behavior" and liable to fines of up to $10,000 and/or suspension.

All that he had expected, but nothing infuriated him more than the totally erroneous reports concerning a driving offense that were put out on an agency wire service and therefore reported, not merely in *The Times* and on BBC television, but in newspapers throughout the world. The reports stated that he had been fined for speeding. That would have been difficult because he wasn't driving—Peter Fleming was. But in a careless piece of reporting that gives journalism a bad name, someone had jumped to the completely unfounded conclusion that as McEnroe was involved—to the extent of being in the car—he must be the culprit. He was beginning to realize just how difficult it was to shake off a bad reputation.

Despite all this, and despite deteriorating relations with the newshounds among the massive Wimbledon press corps, McEnroe buckled down to business in the singles, beating Gullikson in the first round, Raul Ramirez in the second, the great doubles team of Bob Lutz and Stan Smith in a coincidental one-two in rounds three and four, and then the Florida-based South African, Johan Kriek, in the quarters. Ramirez had won a set, and Smith had served and volleyed with the kind of form that won him the title in 1972 before going down 7–5, 3–6, 6–1, 6–2, but there were no more problems for McEnroe in the singles until he met Rod Frawley in the semifinal. That precipitated the second of his run-ins with umpires.

The first had been so publicized that the sequel seemed almost anticlimactic. In his match against Gullikson, at one point McEnroe screamed "You're the pits of the world!" at umpire James, who, in initially jotting down on the card the word "piss" rather than "pits," felt that he could not repeat it when McEnroe demanded to know why he was being penalized for obscenity. "Pits," of course, is not obscene, not even in American vernacular: It merely means "the bottom."

I believe there was a great deal of misunderstanding of the term all over the enclosure. Valerie Burnett, the chairman's wife, thought it meant something much worse and was surprised at the mildness of the term when an American friend explained it to her during the U.S. Open some weeks later. But the incident, compounded by what happened soon afterward in the Frawley match, so firmly entrenched McEnroe as the villain of the piece that many people were inclined to think the worst of everything he did or said.

Certainly his behavior was obnoxious at times—bad enough for the All England Club committee to feel justified in upholding Hoyles' recommendation for the $10,000 fine, which was later reduced to $5,000 by the Pro Council Administrator Marshall Happer, and finally thrown out altogether no less than seven months later when Harry Hopman, McEnroe's choice for the three-man panel drawn up to hear the player's appeal, vetoed it and in doing so carried the day.

The Frawley affair had less serious repercussions but, coming on top of the Gullikson imbroglio, was equally sensational. Rod Frawley, a twenty-eight-year-old Queenslander who had lived and coached in Hamburg for several years before returning to the circuit in 1979, was an unlikely Wimbledon semifinalist. Although he had enjoyed a very successful run on the Grand Prix tour in 1980, his form had been slipping in the months preceding Wimbledon, and his ATP ranking had slumped from 39 to 110. But right from the first round, Rod had settled into a steady rhythm and had always looked the most likely outsider to benefit from the carnage of seeds in the quarter of the draw—Tanner, Vilas, and Pecci all having lost before the third round. In fact, Frawley arrived in the semifinal by way of a highly impressive victory over the promising New Englander Tim Mayotte, having dropped only two sets en route—the same number as McEnroe.

McEnroe should have taken greater heed of all this, but it would have been difficult, given their relative positions in the world rankings, for him not to have gone on court feeling pretty confident. "I knew he had been playing well, but I thought he would be a little nervous to start off," admitted McEnroe. "But instead he goes and breaks my serve in the first game and plays really well. It came as such a surprise that it unnerved me."

In the end, nothing unnerved McEnroe more than the umpire, Wing-Commander George Grimes. When McEnroe yelled out "You're a disgrace to mankind," Grimes instantly assumed that McEnroe was referring to him and gave him a conduct warning. "But I was saying it to myself, umpire," McEnroe called out, his face already contorted with despair and growing anger as another apparent injustice came down on his head. "I was saying 'You're a disgrace to mankind' to *myself*. Aren't I allowed to say that to myself?"

With McEnroe's long record of self-abuse, there is absolutely no reason to doubt his word, but Grimes obviously did not believe him. On his report card he wrote down "McEnroe calls umpire disgrace to mankind."

McEnroe was undoubtedly lucky to escape without some kind of censure, but Wing-Commander Grimes was not entirely blameless. I doubt if senior officers address RAF corporals in the tone that Grimes adopted toward McEnroe, and it is precisely that overbearing and officious attitude which so many of today's generation of players resent so strongly. The fact that it was Borg, a much respected rival, whom McEnroe faced in the final was, in my opinion, not the only reason for his vastly improved behavior. A major factor was the umpiring of the Welshman Bob Jenkins, whose calm, low-key manner struck precisely the right note of unruffled authority.

So once again the conduct problem overshadowed the tennis in McEnroe's semifinal, which was a pity because Frawley proved himself a worthy opponent and, showing not the slightest sign of being overawed by the occasion, challenged the American through three hard-fought sets with solid serve-and-volley tennis before going down 7–6, 6–4, 7–5.

The other semifinal had been a classic—"A Banquet for the Gods" announced the London *Times* in a rare moment of euphoria—and indeed Borg had to scurry around to find his very best recipes before he could get the better of Connors, who, as his Las Vegas friends would say, was really cookin'. Sixteen aces helped Borg pull back from a two-set deficit—the first time that anyone had got him in that much trouble since Mark Edmondson in 1977.

The very act of survival against such an inspired opponent only heightened the aura of Borg's invincibility at Wimbledon and increased the feeling among many pundits that he would extend his incredible run of title-winning years to six. But despite everything that had gone before, McEnroe also had his supporters, especially among those who simply felt that a change would be good for the overall health of the game. I personally was convinced he could win—I had seen him beat Borg often enough on cement and Supreme courts, so why not on grass?

To hope for a repeat of the drama and excellence of the final of the previous year was asking too much, and in that we were proved right. Even compared with the Borg-Connors semifinal, the 1981 final was a less tasty feast, but it was close enough and technically good enough to live alongside some of the best Wimbledon finals of recent years. In retrospect, Borg was a little lucky to still be in front by the time the second set reached 6–all. The Swede had taken the first on a single service break, but McEnroe had reached break point on the champion's serve no less than eight times in four separate service games.

The first tie-break rather confirmed what the score had thus far failed to do—namely, that the five-time champion was losing control of the match. With McEnroe coming up with precision volleys and cleverly disguised lobs, Borg managed to win only one tie-break point before the American set course for victory by leveling the match 4–6, 7–6.

Borg led 3–1 in the third set, but McEnroe, chipping his return low

to Borg's feet, broke back in the seventh game and then survived an onslaught on his own delivery in the tenth that proved to be Borg's last real hope of salvaging his crown. With the Centre Court crowd—as noisy as any I have heard in a final—helping to raise the tension level to new heights, Björn produced an unbelievable backhand pass as he raced onto a good, deep volley from McEnroe and reached the first of four set-points. Earning his spurs as a prospective champion, McEnroe survived and took the match into another tie-break. A beautiful floated cross-court pass off the forehand deprived the Swede of one service-point and a backhand, chipped deep down the line, took away another. They were strokes of exquisite skill and timing—the strokes of a man worthy to hold the game's premier title. Maybe, deep down inside him, Borg sensed that too, for although he fought bravely in the fourth set, he was playing like a man searching for miracles, and McEnroe, controlled and resolute, didn't have any on offer. So by the score of 4–6, 7–6, 7–6, 6–4 a new king was enthroned, ending a long and dignified reign.

It was not viewed as a very happy coronation within the hallowed halls of the All England Club. The ridiculous failure to communicate properly over the invitation to the Champion's Dinner only emphasized the fact that there was little love lost between Wimbledon and its new champion. And that was the saddest thing of all. It was sad, too, to hear a friend like Dan Maskell, the BBC's veteran commentator, tell me, "I found McEnroe's behavior so offensive that it completely ruined my enjoyment of this year's Wimbledon."

As there is no one who has a greater or more abiding love for the game than Maskell, nor indeed many with a deeper knowledge of it, such opinions must be respected. It is not just a question of the old school being unable to cope with the brave new world. Maskell frequently enjoyed and defended Ilie Nastase. But McEnroe, in his rage for perfection and intolerance of injustice, takes matters to a stage that many quite reasonable people find unacceptable. John simply didn't realize that to start with, although I know that he does now.

But to paint him as the sole villain in the sad saga of his bittersweet Wimbledon triumph would be too easy and too dangerous for the future health of the game. The All England Club needs to take a long, hard and self-critical look at its own role in the unfortunate affair, for reasons that I will now try to explain.

Opposite: Unloved? McEnroe doesn't seem to be the only person in ecstasy as he reacts to the winning match point against Björn Borg in the 1981 Wimbledon final. *Popperfoto*

109

10

THE DINNER

The extent to which the All England Club has lost touch with the present-day generation of tennis professionals was never more clearly or sadly illustrated than by the absurd failure of communication that resulted in the new champion's nonappearance at the Champion's Dinner after Wimbledon 1981.

First, let me lay out the facts as best I know them—facts that, for the most part, were buried or at least partly obscured in the national press for the next few days, as yet another load of what Frank Keating once described in the London *Guardian* as "headline writers' graffiti" dubbed McEnroe as ill-mannered, ungracious, a slob and worse.

After the final, John McEnroe had three conversations in the Wimbledon dressing room concerning the dinner: two with club secretary Chris Gorringe and one with his father. At first, both John and his father were under the impression that it was still more of a ball-type affair than a dinner, with the male and female champion expected to open the dancing together. In issuing the verbal invitation—apparently the champion receives no written invitation or details of when and where he is expected to show up—Gorringe apprised McEnroe of the details in the first conversation and spoke to him again after the press interviews. It was then that McEnroe asked if it would be all right for him to bring a party of eight friends. Gorringe said that this might be difficult, as three places at the top table and two at the table nearby would probably be all they could manage. According to Gorringe, McEnroe "found this hard to understand."

Meanwhile John McEnroe, Sr., had been telling a nationwide audience in America, when he was interviewed live on NBC television, that the whole family would be attending the Champion's Dinner that evening. "At this stage there was never any doubt in my mind that we would be going," Mr. McEnroe told me. "Although I was still unclear as to the exact nature of the function, I had mentioned it to John when I congratulated him in the dressing room right after the match, just to verify his intention of attending, and he said, 'Yes, sure. That's fine.'"

However, the final conversation between the champion and Gorringe had been less conclusive, and by the time Mr. and Mrs. McEnroe arrived back at Blake's Hotel, neither father nor son knew exactly when they were supposed to show up or how many people they could take.

"I phoned John at his flat, and he told me he really didn't know what was going on and would I find out," Mr. McEnroe went on. "He was having a pretty good party with a group of buddies, so I agreed to call Wimbledon and let him know."

Getting no immediate answer from the main Wimbledon switchboard, and realizing that everyone was probably watching the mixed doubles final, which was still in progress, Mr. McEnroe then dialed the referee's office and began a series of conversations with former British Davis Cup player Alan Mills, who is now assistant referee at the championships. Although Mills had absolutely nothing to do with the organization of the dinner, he agreed to find out what he could from the secretary's office.

Three or four phone calls were then made, and both John McEnroe, Sr., and Alan Mills have, in independent talks with me, agreed that the following points were raised: Mr. McEnroe, wanting to know "the drill," as he put it, was told the details of dress and venue (the Savoy), but Mills warned that the time might be put back, as the dinner could not start until the chairman arrived; and as the mixed was still in progress as they spoke, everything might be delayed. The subject of John, Jr., bringing eight friends does not seem to have been raised again, but his father did make two points to Mills. First, he wanted to know whether it would be permissible for John to arrive "at dessert or coffee time" to say his few words, and second, would it be possible for an Irish couple who were guests of Mr. and Mrs. McEnroe in London to come along.

Mills said he would relay those questions and get back to him. The answers virtually assured that Chris Evert Lloyd would be the only champion attending the dinner that night. The invitations, Mills was instructed to say, were for the family only, and if John could not be there for the entire dinner, which was now due to start at 10:30 P.M., the invitation "was respectfully withdrawn."

Although Chris Gorringe skirted that particular issue in a fairly detailed written reply to certain questions I put to him, also in writing, Mills is adamant that he was instructed to use that phrase.

"I was absolutely incredulous," Mr. McEnroe told me. "I asked Mills if he was absolutely certain of what he was saying and if, under the circumstances, it might not be better for someone from the committee to call me direct so that there would be no misunderstanding. I just couldn't believe it—and, I might add, I am not referring to the two extra seats, although not being able to squeeze in two more in the entourage of the champion at a dinner for some two hundred people didn't seem to make much sense either. But that was not a stumbling block. Our friends would have understood and met us later for drinks or whatever. But insisting that the champion sit through a formal two-hour dinner making small talk to people he barely knew was beyond my comprehension."

Mills agreed to double-check and eventually called back himself, confirming that if John was not there by a specific time, the invitation was "respectfully withdrawn."

"So I presume I know what the answer is going to be," Mills said at the end of their final conversation, which throughout had been conducted in relatively friendly and informal tones.

"Well, I don't know what the answer is," Mr. McEnroe replied. "But I do think the whole thing is absolutely ridiculous."

He then relayed the details of his conversation with Mills and his feelings on the subject to John and told him that, considering the terms being laid down by the All England Club, he should no longer feel he had an obligation to go.

"Now, with the benefit of hindsight, it would have been better to have gone through with my original plan," Mr. McEnroe told me. "That would have entailed Kay and me and the boys going along at the required time, apologizing for John's tardiness and slipping out to give him a call to say 'Come on over' at the appropriate moment. I'm sure it would have worked out better that way."

However, having had it made clear that the McEnroe family also would not be welcome if their son did not show up at the prescribed hour, Mr. McEnroe's initial eagerness to seek a compromise had cooled considerably. To say the least, he was indignant and angry. Faced with the option of remaining with a small group of close friends or dressing up to face a potentially hostile audience, stuck between officials of a club that had just handed him a $10,000 fine, the new champion did the human thing, and stayed home.

So much for the facts of the matter. Personally, I find the whole episode beyond belief. Why was it left to the champion's father and the assistant referee to forage for details that were wholly the responsibility of the All England Club committee? Why, in an organization that prides itself, quite rightly, on its efficiency and attention to detail, was an important invitation so casually, tardily and sloppily handled? And, most pertinently of all, why did the chairman, Sir Brian Burnett, and his committee sit around at the dinner, tut-tutting and looking at their watches long after their self-imposed deadline had passed, as if they

Opposite: The new Wimbledon champion—before the disputes over the Champions' Dinner. *E. L. Scott*

still expected to see John McEnroe walk through the door? Knowing what they knew, namely that they themselves had withdrawn the invitation, wasn't it somewhat deceitful to keep that very stringent condition on which the invitation had become based a secret? Weren't they, deliberately or not, ensuring that McEnroe would be made to look a bigger villain than he really was?

I wonder if Chris Evert Lloyd, who in her typically gracious fashion felt the need to apologize for John's absence when she spoke at the dinner, would have felt the same way had she known of the ultimatum.

According to Chris Gorringe, in his written reply, the reason it was left to Alan Mills to deal with Mr. McEnroe's queries was "at that particular time the Mixed Doubles Final was about to finish and the Royal Box had the Duke and Duchess of Kent present and, therefore, the Chairman and myself needed to be at that point for the presentation of prizes, etc."

Fair enough, but was everybody so busy during the course of the next hour or so that they couldn't find the time to pick up the phone and call Mr. McEnroe direct? For that matter, would it have been so terribly demeaning for Sir Brian Burnett himself to have walked into his own dressing room after the final and spoken personally with his new champion? If Sir Brian does not consider it demeaning to talk to tennis players, then I can only say that he acts as if he does. He even acts that way with their fathers.

When John McEnroe, Sr., came to Wimbledon in 1980 to spend the whole fortnight with his son for the first time, he was not quite prepared for the cold and offhand way in which he was received:

"No one had warned me about the way things are done at Wimbledon. I suppose I had been spoiled by the reception I had received at other major championships. In Paris, Philippe Chatrier, who, after all, is president of the International Federation, had gone out of his way to make Kay and myself feel at home, and it was the same most other places. I have no illusions as to why we were treated so well. Obviously it was because we were the parents of John McEnroe. But I must say it came as a bit of a shock when my initial request for a locker-room pass for myself—remember John has no coach with him like the other top players—and a grounds pass for Mark, so that we could help John with all the little things that need attending to, was turned down. Eventually I got a pass into the locker room but only for the second week."

If Mr. McEnroe quickly realized that personal invitations to dinner of the type he had received from Chatrier in Paris would not be forthcoming in London, he did make an attempt, in his capacity as father and manager of the No. 2 seed, to establish some kind of contact with Chatrier's equivalent, Sir Brian Burnett.

"I told Chris Gorringe that I would be happy to meet with Sir Brian anytime, anywhere at his own convenience," Mr. McEnroe told me. The immediate reply he received was that the chairman was unable to see him "because he was entertaining royalty." And he heard nothing more.

If John McEnroe can rightly be accused of saying some damn silly things in the heat of the moment on a tennis court, I have found none sillier, nor more calculated to give offense, than that official reply offered on behalf of Air Chief Marshal Burnett.

But I only use it as an example. There are various forms of rudeness—the up-front, flagrant, shouting type of abuse that comes pouring out of people when they are in a temper and the snotty-nosed, supercilious, terribly calm kind of put-down that the British employ so well. I don't like either very much, but if Wimbledon takes the extraordinary steps of withholding membership from a champion for the first time in its history, as it did, because he is ill-mannered (behavior, after all, is the basis of the charge), then its members cannot expect their own manners to escape scrutiny. Although in the twenty-one years that I have reported the championships, a wide range of people such as Fred Hoyles, committeemen like Jonathan Avory and Humphrey Truman and Chris Gorringe himself, have been unfailingly courteous and helpful, I have also been confronted with appalling rudeness and bad manners from people who now appear to be setting themselves up as guardians of etiquette.

It is amazing how the British allow a coat and tie and the right accent to camouflage deficiencies in character. History is littered with examples of "gentlemen" who turned out to be cads or sometimes even traitors. And, of course, the opposite is equally true. Sloppy dress and an inability to maintain the stiff upper lip in public are immediate black marks against anyone trying to enter a gentlemen's club. The pity of it is that, in excluding John McEnroe, the All England Club has denied membership to one of the most highly principled and morally straight young men ever to wear the Wimbledon crown.

But humbug and hypocrisy—both useful social passports in any number of upper-crust societies—are emollients McEnroe's thin skin cannot tolerate. When Fred Hoyles, a Lincolnshire farmer who is possibly too nice and gentle a man to deal with the fiery temperaments of today's superstars, tried to shake hands with McEnroe at one stage during Wimbledon in a gesture of "no hard feelings," the result was a collision of two totally different upbringings. John was genuinely appalled.

"How can he expect me to shake his hand?" McEnroe asked incredulously. "I called him names; he's hit me with fines—we're not exactly

Kay McEnroe looking suitably proud about the men in her life.

friends, that's for sure. So why try and make out we are? It's so hypocritical."

That kind of attitude doesn't make life any easier, but I think I prefer it to the insincerity of a smile you can never trust.

But that is peculiarly a McEnroe problem. For the sake of Wimbledon and its deserved reputation as the greatest tennis tournament in the world, as well as for the overall health of the game in Britain, I hope that Sir Brian and his committee quickly and drastically alter their attitude toward the players. The public support that Wimbledon received amidst the hysteria of the 1973 ATP boycott will not be revived if, individually, top players start bypassing the championships simply because they can find something better to do. And there are already signs that they may.

Eliot Teltscher, now firmly established among the world's top ten, has not played at Wimbledon for three years because of the way in which he considers the players are treated. "Everybody there thinks they are above the players," Teltscher told Linda Pentz in a *Tennis Week* interview. "They should realize that if it were not for the players, they wouldn't have an event."

As I reported in the *Guardian* in November 1981, Vitas Gerulaitis has gone on record as saying that he only plays at Wimbledon because his clothing and racket contracts stipulate that he must. Ivan Lendl, who is starting to challenge McEnroe for the position of No. 1 in the world, dislikes the tournament for reasons quite separate from the problems that he encounters in playing on grass.

So it must be realized that McEnroe is merely a symbol of a deeper and more widespread antipathy that has been festering for some years toward the club. I find it very sad but not particularly surprising. In their military manner, the All England officials—and I include the majority of umpires—tend to treat the players as foot soldiers who must do or die and never query an officer's decision. Like it or not, self-made millionaires from foreign lands do not take kindly to being drafted into Queen Victoria's army.

As Clive Bernstein at the Queen's Club and Len Owen of Benson & Hedges have shown, it is quite possible to secure the trust and cooperation of these supposedly spoiled superstars if one takes a little trouble to find out what makes them tick and treats them intelligently. "There is no doubt that McEnroe is suspicious of officialdom, but it is all a question of how you approach him," Owen explains. "I have found that he is much more at ease if you catch him at an informal, offbeat moment, metaphorically if not actually wearing your sweater and jeans rather than blazer and badge. He always gives you a straight answer, always fulfills his commitments and is obviously a tremendous asset to our tournament."

The cynics may point out that, as a commercial promoter, it is Owen's job to keep McEnroe happy. Quite true. But my point is that Sir Brian Burnett has an equal, if not greater, responsibility to make a similar effort to ensure that today's top players feel comfortable and content when they are playing at Wimbledon. Sir Brian's responsibilities in that area are wider than Len Owen's because, unlike Wembley, which only makes a profit for Benson & Hedges, Wimbledon is virtually the sole benefactor and provider of life-sustaining funds for the Lawn Tennis Association and, through it, the grass roots of the game in Britain.

I am not suggesting that Wimbledon should fawn before all and sundry and turn a blind eye to the excesses of on-court behavior as perpetuated by McEnroe and other lesser players whose conduct on outside courts often passes unnoticed. But I am saying that it is pigheaded and totally unnecessary to allow a situation to exist whereby the club chairman doesn't even feel comfortable enough to walk up to his champion and invite him to dinner. What I find most puzzling is the bloody-minded intransigence with which the All England Club has pursued the McEnroe affair. Everybody, including the player himself, agrees that he behaved very badly on two or three occasions and that he might well have been defaulted in the first round. It is also generally accepted that he was lucky to escape unpunished after the original fine of $10,000 had been reduced to $5,000 by Pro Council Administrator Marshall Happer and then thrown out altogether as a result of a minority veto on the arbitration panel. None of that is in serious dispute. But why was it necessary to reject out of hand the feeler put out in the summer of 1981 by John McEnroe, Sr., through ATP Executive Director Butch Buchholz suggesting some kind of a truce with concessions on both sides? Why wasn't the All England Club prepared to at least talk about it? Why couldn't Sir Brian Burnett have made an informal approach to Mr. McEnroe when he attended the U.S. Open in New York so that the pair of them could open up a basic line of communication? If there is any benefit to be gained from Wimbledon waging a war of stony silence with its champion, it escapes me.

Obviously some solution must be found, and there is one readily available if the All England Club is really interested in heading off a disastrous situation. Presuming that Sir Brian is either too shy or too proud to disentangle himself from his royal duties and to muck in occasionally down in the dressing room, some young, active British professionals who are already members of the club must be co-opted onto the committee to act as direct and effective links between the players and the hierarchy. The obvious candidates are Roger Taylor, Richard Lewis (an ideal choice because he is already a member of the ATP board), John Feaver and Robin Drysdale. Only in that way will the gulf of distrust be bridged and so enable Wimbledon to reap the full benefits of all the truly fine efforts that have been made with modernization of the club facilities. It might also enable the current generation of players to look back with gratitude at the deeds of Sir Brian's predecessor, Herman David, whose courage and foresight in 1968 forced open tennis on a reluctant amateur world. It would be pleasing, too, if an atmosphere existed in which both champions could attend and enjoy the Champion's Dinner—with their friends.

11

U.S. OPEN HAT TRICK

In less than four minutes on a blustery afternoon at Flushing Meadow in September 1981, John McEnroe uncorked four knockout blows that finally and irrevocably stripped the mantle of supremacy from Björn Borg's shoulders. The score in the final of the U.S. Open stood at one set all and 4–3 to Borg in the third, with the Swede's serve to come. For the first time in a fluctuating and far from error-free match, Borg was starting to find an easy rhythm and his baseline drives, and the packed Stadium Court crowd of twenty thousand was giving him every encouragement as he glided toward a two set to one lead.

Then suddenly McEnroe turned everything inside out. Five points later McEnroe was a different player and we were watching a different match. John admitted afterward that the way he played that game made him feel as if he could hit any shot he wanted. Those who saw it could understand why.

McEnroe won four of those five points with outright winners: the first was a scorching backhand cross-court pass on the return of serve; the second a topspin lob deep into Borg's backhand corner that the Swede, caught very close to the net, never bothered to chase. They were both exquisite shots that would have been difficult to reproduce at any stage. But, after allowing Borg one point, the defending champion produced both instantly, in sequence, as if he were providing his own live version of instant replay: backhand pass; topspin lob. Borg looked stunned, and no wonder. Even he, who has taken a longer, closer look at McEnroe's talent these past few years than anyone else in the game, was shocked by the streak of genius that had just flashed before him. The power of one shot and the precision of the other, each repeated in perfect harmony at a crucial, pivotal moment of the match, revealed a rare and instinctive gift shared only by the greatest champions. Borg has that gift and, seeing it so clearly and so cruelly reflected in his opponent's play, made it that much more psychologically damaging.

Borg never recovered. Two games later a stinging forehand winner clinched the set 6–4 for McEnroe. Any chance Björn had of getting back into a match that he had seemed to be on the point of controlling just a few minutes earlier was destroyed by the deft manner in which the American took the pace off his shots, forcing constant reprogramming of the Borg computer as each stroke came back at different levels and different speeds, doctored with varying amounts of spin.

Rod Laver, one of many former champions present for the Centennial Celebration of the USTA, was impressed, and McEnroe would want no better stamp of approval. Laver noted, in particular, the champion's footwork—that precious ability to meet any shot, no matter how hard it is hit, with perfect balance even after being forced to change direction.

And so McEnroe joined Bill Tilden as the only other man since World War I to have claimed the U.S. singles crown in three successive years. His 4–6, 6–2, 6–4, 6–3 victory was a crushing defeat for Borg, who had failed once again to win the one major title that had always eluded him. Untypically he stalked off court without waiting for the prize-giving ceremony and admitted to me, when we met in Geneva just a few weeks later, that it had been a deliberate act. "I was just very, very disappointed," Borg said honestly. "I couldn't face the idea of making a nice speech in front of all those people. I suppose I was a bad boy."

But for McEnroe, of course, it was a triumph. Apart from his exciting and often tempestuous five-set semifinal with friend and neighbor Vitas Gerulaitis, in which the CBS courtside mike took a hammering from the McEnroe racket and the officials took a hammering from the Gerulaitis mouth, only the silkily skillful Indian Ramesh Krishnan had given McEnroe any real trouble. Krishnan, whose father was a Wimbledon semifinalist twice in the sixties, served for a two set to love lead before McEnroe realized there was serious work to be done and battled his way out of trouble 6–7, 7–6, 6–4, 6–2.

When Heinz Gunthardt of Switzerland was unable to partner Peter McNamara in the doubles final because of illness, McEnroe and Peter Fleming won the title by default. But they had already played a match worthy of the final one round earlier when a pair of veteran Aussies called John Newcombe and Fred Stolle forced them to battle for five long sets before going down 7–6 in the fifth. The crowd loved every minute of it, mainly because the two old pros milked the situation for every drop of entertainment value it was worth, while the young Americans angrily refused to see the joke. Inevitably they were a long way from winning any popularity contest, and if this was to be a contest of heroes and villains, the die became cast when McEnroe hit

Peter Fleming and John McEnroe in action during a doubles match. *Popperfoto*

Robert Evans, standing in for Anthony Harvey as director on his own production of the film *Players,* explains the finer points of acting to John McEnroe, who had a cameo part in a scene at Caesars Palace in Las Vegas with Pancho Gonzales. *Richard Evans*

Stolle at close range with a full-blooded drive and then took a long time raising his hand in a gesture of apology.

"But that wasn't where he lost me," said Stolle, who, through his association with Gerulaitis, had come to know McEnroe pretty well, especially after John took an apartment at Turnberry Isle in Florida where Fred directs the tennis activities. "Being hit was no big deal, despite what everyone said afterward. I would probably have played the same shot. No, what I couldn't stomach was his sarcastic attitude when I pointed to a mark left by one of Peter's serves that had landed wide. John was at the net like myself, and when I touched the spot with my racket just to verify that the linesman's call was correct, he said, 'Oh yea, Fred, why not pick any mark? Any old mark will do.' That was where he lost me."

It was a sad and familiar story. Off court, McEnroe would never seriously suggest that Fred Stolle would try to con anyone out of a point. But on court, in the heat of the battle, rational thinking becomes obliterated by a paranoid conviction that everyone is trying to do him in. It was to be that way frequently during the remaining months of 1981, and it was only after the Volvo Masters in the following January that he realized that it was not just his reputation but his actual play that was beginning to suffer. In the intervening months, however, more friendships were to be put under needless strain.

12

SYDNEY

Fatigue was becoming a factor by the time McEnroe arrived in Sydney to defend his Custom Credit Australian Indoor title at the Hordern Pavilion. Most of the previous week had been spent in Melbourne, recovering from a heavy dose of jet lag after a wild dash from the Davis Cup semifinal in Portland, Oregon, and competing, in some fashion or other, in the Mazda Super Challenge—a lavishly organized, nationally televised exhibition that carried big money.

It is unlikely that McEnroe was able, either physically or emotionally, to give the Mazda his undivided attention. He was there because he had given a commitment to promoter John Brown. But he probably wished he hadn't. Once again a good promoter with a tournament and, even better, guaranteed money had come up with an offer that at a distance seemed too good to refuse. But when the reality of such an offer looms closer, even staggering money does not seem adequate compensation for having to rush for another plane and try to perform in a different hemisphere less than thirty hours after giving just about everything you have to give for your country in a Davis Cup tie.

McEnroe knows he overcommits himself but he never reneges on a promise, and when Jimmy Connors pulled out of the Mazda with one of his indefinable illnesses, John knew he would be needed in Melbourne more than ever. But even if a willing horse leads himself to the water and laps at it in a gesture of goodwill, there is no way he can create a thirst that isn't there.

Although it had the trappings of a big event, the Mazda was nothing more than an eight-man round-robin exhibition with some extra money added for the winner, in addition to the large sums guaranteed to all those who showed up. With no Volvo Grand Prix or ATP points, and no particular prestige outside its own immediate area, the Mazda was something less than a Super Challenge for McEnroe.

The thirst for victory was to return with a vengeance in Sydney the following week, but in Melbourne there were other needs to attend to—like sleep and relaxation. There were reports of McEnroe actually laughing on court and of nights on the town with the beautiful star of an American movie that was being shot in the area. Given the circumstances it was impossible for him to compete at his customary pitch and, sure enough, he lost twice in the round-robin format, the second time to Gene Mayer, who always seems to be able to utilize his considerable talents when there is nothing much at stake. Mayer, who went on to win the Mazda title, is very nearly as talented as McEnroe. In fact, now that Nastase is no longer a major force in the game, no one other than McEnroe has such instinctive touch and variety of shots as the younger of the Mayer brothers. (Sandy, a more orthodox performer, who reached the Wimbledon semifinal in the ATP boycott year of 1973, climbed back into the top fifteen on the computer after an excellent finish in 1981.)

But unhappily for Gene's kindly Hungarian-born father, who has coached both his sons and who so desperately wants them to play to their full potential, there is one decisive difference between Gene Mayer and John McEnroe. Gene can't win the big titles. Incredibly for a man who has been ranked as high as No. 4 in the world, he had never, up to the end of 1981, even reached the *semi*final of a Grand Slam tournament. But his talent is such that in an event like the Mazda, with McEnroe below par, it is Mayer who looks and plays like the No. 1 in the world.

The Custom Credit Australian Indoors, a $175,000 Super Series stop on the year-long Volvo Grand Prix tour, was, however, a different matter. While Mayer sped off to Europe in search of more exhibition money, McEnroe got down to the serious business of living up to his newfound image of the player who must never lose.

That is what the pressure of being No. 1 is all about. Every time the player recognized as being the No. 1 in the world comes off court in a Grand Prix event having lost, he has to face a roomful of reporters who will ask in a chorus, "What's wrong?" The answer that, on this particular day, the other guy played better is not acceptable to them. The press want absolutes, even if they disregard reality. The No. 1 is No. 1 because he is better than the others, right? Therefore he should always beat the others, right? So what's wrong?

It is, of course, not that simple. There are at least fifty other players out there who are quite capable of beating anybody on their day, depending on the surface and general playing conditions as well, of course, as the overall condition of "Mr. Invincible" who is supposed to win. As is now clear, not even Borg is a machine—a revelation that must have disappointed Saab, who probably thought they had found a new prototype when they signed him to a sponsorship contract.

So it is quite possible for the No. 1 in the world to lose occasionally along the way. And when he does, it usually seems to come as an unfathomable shock to the local press who, logically enough, are only interested in what happens in *their* city and are not impressed by excuses borne in or en route from faraway places. McEnroe realizes this and is particularly sensitive to the need to do justice to the coveted position to which he aspired the moment that he beat Borg at Flushing Meadow. Losing to Bill Scanlon in the TransAmerica Open in San Francisco two weeks after his triumph at the U.S. Open had been a severe blow to his pride. I realized how much it had stung him when he started talking to me about it in Portland.

"I was really embarrassed," he muttered. "I realized afterward that I was the only person who had done really well at the Open who had not gone on to win a title the next time out. Björn won his Grand Prix event in Geneva, Tracy won her tournament on the women's tour, but I go and bomb out in San Francisco. That was a real downer, man. Scanlon played well but I hate playing the guy and I should never have lost to him."

Pride was the only emotion that generated that little outburst which came straight from the heart. To hell with the money and the points: both are important in the long haul but here, at a specific moment that was important to him psychologically in the continuing rivalry with his peers, he had failed to live up to the dizzying heights of perfection he had set himself. The very fact that it hurt him as much as it did provides one of the vital clues in the search for the component parts of McEnroe's greatness. Genius that blossoms from extraordinary athletic skill and dexterity with a racket is a useful asset for the prospective champion, but several have made it all the way to the top without one or the other. John Newcombe, Stan Smith and Jan Kodes, among the more recent Wimbledon Champions, are examples. But no one ever made it to the top without pride. All the talent in the world cannot fill the void if pride is missing.

McEnroe was determined not to let another lapse occur in Sydney. So, after the merriment of Melbourne, the business of winning took precedence over everything when McEnroe checked into the Kingsgate Hyatt, a towerlike structure whose neon signs acts as a kind of beacon at night for the salacious pleasures that lie below it. Known throughout Australia simply as The Cross, the area of King's Cross is highlighted by a short strip of gaudy glitter running the length of Dailingshurst Road that can be mentioned in the same breath as Soho or Pigalle. Strip clubs, massage parlors, pubs, restaurants and late-night cafés run by the Greek, Italian and Yugoslav immigrants, who have given Sydney a much-needed cosmopolitan flavor, offer just about

McEnroe usually quite enjoyed press conferences with Australian tennis writers during the Custom Credit Indoors. But there were moments . . . *Richard Evans*

everything a lonely heart could desire. But McEnroe is not the sort of person who enjoys a cheap thrill. And it is not merely because he can afford more expensive pleasures that he shuns the kind of adventures so many young men find irresistible. Perhaps it would be taking it too far to describe McEnroe as puritanical, but as we have intimated earlier in this story, a quick encounter with a buxom blonde in a massage parlor is simply not his idea of fun.

That is not to say, however, that he turned his back on Sydney night life completely. Just a few hundred yards from the Hyatt, away from the neon lights of The Cross, there is a rather smart restaurant and discotheque called The Cauldron. Later in the week, with a few victories under his belt, McEnroe was to spend time there and experience encounters of a different kind.

But first there was tennis to be played. Brad Drewett, the Australian left-hander with the flowing blond hair, was John's first-round opponent; and although Brad never served well enough to offer serious resistance, there were familiar signs of tension in the air even at this early stage. The Hordern Pavilion, situated right next to the famous Sydney Cricket Ground where the World Youth Soccer Cup was in progress, is a small, intimate arena that seats fewer than four thousand people for tennis. The players and the public keep close and distracting company. And, of course, those distractions become magnified when a player as highly strung as McEnroe is performing in front of an audience that consists, in large part, of voluble Australians quaffing beer and nibbling at meals being served to them in courtside boxes by teams of pretty, overworked waitresses.

It did not take long for McEnroe to lay down the law. "Nobody move until *after* the game, all right?" he exclaimed loudly at the beginning of the second set and then, assessing the situation with a customary dose of poetic license, added, "Forty-five people move after every point!"

One thing no one was doing was popping beer cans, because McEnroe had laid down that law behind the scenes long before the matches started. Drawing on his experiences of the year before, McEnroe had made an extraordinary yet somehow typical request, to which the startled catering manager had acceded as the lesser of two evils (the greater one being the prospect of an enraged No. 1 seed screaming at a thirsty Australian approximately once every three minutes). As a result all the cans of beer—without which your average Aussie finds it quite impossible to sit through a sporting event—were being popped open outside the arena before they were served. It might have dawned on John McEnroe when that "request" was granted that his skill with a racket, allied of course to a certain temper, had enabled him to succeed in a task many would not even have considered worth attempting—namely, to change, ever so slightly, the beer-drinking habits of an Australian crowd. Down Under that is known as having influence.

So with the crowd sentenced to sip in silence, McEnroe and, indeed, the majority of players were left with the one major distraction that tarnished the image of Graham Lovett's efficiently run event—bad officiating. Yes, it was an old story, but for the first few days in Sydney, poor line-calling and umpiring that was not competent enough to justify the officious tone in which it was conducted wrote a particularly dark chapter into this essentially repetitive tale of horror.

The gravity of the situation was sensed when Ross Case and Syd Ball, a couple of true-blue Aussies who have always accepted the rough and the smooth of life on the tour with equanimity, both warned the press after their first-round match that if the standard of officiating did not improve, eruptions were inevitable once the less tolerant star names got into the act. And sure enough, McEnroe and Rod Frawley, staging a repeat of their Wimbledon semifinal, proved them right.

This time, however, it was Frawley, a thoughtful professional not usually given to outrageous acts of indiscretion, who reacted in unprecedented fashion to a series of bad line calls by deliberately setting a trap for Kevin Bolton, secretary of the Australian Umpires Association. With McEnroe leading 3–1 and 40–15 in the first set of their second-round match, Frawley pretended to disagree with an "out" call on a McEnroe serve. When Bolton went along with the ruse and had the call changed, Frawley turned on the umpire and accused him of succumbing to player intimidation. This is a frequent gripe heard among the quieter players, who feel that the loudmouths eventually start getting points that do not belong to them as nervous officials give them the benefit of the doubt every time there is a close call. As far as the frustrated Frawley was concerned, he had just proved his point. But being a basically fair man, Frawley did not feel particularly proud of himself afterward.

"Of course I was wrong to do it," Rod admitted as he poured out his feelings on the subject at a riveting press conference. "But after the injustices I have suffered these past two weeks, I just wanted to make an example of him. I was challenging the guy's competence and he fell for it. Like most of the officiating in Australia this season, it was a disgrace."

Despite the fact that Frawley's ploy had worked in his favor, McEnroe joined the Queenslander in demanding that the umpire be replaced. But after some heated exchanges, referee Bill Gilmour, who was to learn more about the rough edge of McEnroe's tongue two weeks later in Tokyo, stood by his official and ordered the players to continue.

The previous week in his hometown of Brisbane, Frawley had lost a tight three-set match to Mark Edmondson in the semifinal of a Grand Prix event when a serve from Edmondson, which was clearly long, had been called "good" on match point.

"I've never known officiating as bad as this," Frawley continued. "I'll turn into a McEnroe myself if it goes on. These guys should practice line-calling just like we have to practice our play. Do you think we would be able to play as well as we do if we didn't spend hours on the practice court? Then why should officials think they can come into a Grand Prix event and start calling serves traveling at over one hundred miles an hour as if they have been doing it all year? Yes, I know they are part-timers, but that makes the need to practice all the more imperative. There's too much at stake for the players to get screwed while they get their act together."

Frawley was making a highly pertinent point and one that McEnroe, echoing much the same sentiments, readily endorsed. If McEnroe's objections to officiating mistakes had been largely anticipated, the vehemence of the criticism leveled at umpires and linesmen by Australia's own players had caused widespread consternation. As we have seen, it is far from being solely an Australian problem, but at least the furor—intensified a week later when Vitas Gerulaitis resolutely refused to return to the court during the final of a Grand Prix tournament in Melbourne and was consequently defaulted—spurred people into action. Lovett, as conscientious a tournament director as one could find, persuaded his sponsors, Custom Credit, to put up between five and ten thousand Australian dollars as a contribution toward a fund to finance the training of court officials. With Brian Tobin, Australia's representative on the Pro Council, also voicing his concern, it is to be hoped that Australia will lead the way in producing a new breed of officials who can do their job with sufficient skill to avoid antagonizing an increasingly suspicious and intolerant generation of players.

There is no question in my mind that the players are at fault as soon as they start abusing officials, no matter what mistakes have been made. But that does not mean that they should be ordered around by people who are simply not competent enough to do their jobs. Gerulaitis has often behaved inexcusably on a tennis court, but his rationale for refusing to continue his final against Peter McNamara in Melbourne was hard to argue with. Calls toward the end of the tight third set had become so bad that McNamara had actually asked the umpire to reverse a decision in Vitas' favor, even though it meant giving the American match point. Apparently both the umpire and the net judge had failed to notice that the ball had passed *through* the net rather than over it! It was after he had missed the match point and become the victim of yet another highly dubious decision that Gerulaitis decided to refuse to play on until the umpire was changed. When this request was refused, Vitas sat tight in his chair and allowed himself to be counted out on the clock.

A few days afterward, Vitas, who has been in just as many scraps with officialdom in his time as McEnroe, was still making sense on the subject when he talked to me about it:

"If I had gone back on court and lost, it would have been sour grapes, and if I had gone back on and won, everyone would have said, 'You won so why are you complaining?' I wanted to win badly but this problem is too important. As players we are bound by a set of rules. Yet what rule says professional athletes have to stand around in silence, accepting totally incompetent officiating? I mean, when two guys can't tell whether the ball has gone through the net or over it, you've got a problem, believe me.

"In Australia, just as in England, most officials are too old. That's not an attack on old people—it's just a fact of life. I'd like to go on playing top-class tennis till I'm sixty, but I'm just not going to be able to. Nobody's going to say, 'Oh, poor old Vitas, let him continue because he needs free lunch tickets.' But that's the attitude in many umpires' associations. It's got to change, and I hope what I did in Melbourne will make people realize it."

In their different ways Frawley and Gerulaitis had both made extraordinary, eye-catching stands against the bane of the tennis pro's life—bad officiating. Neither had done it in the way that the establishment would have wished. Neither had derived much satisfaction or pleasure from what he had done. But, unintentionally, both had lent credence to McEnroe's screams for justice. Their actions, although not entirely correct, had taken a more concrete and substantive form of protest than McEnroe's frequently misunderstood rantings. For once The Great Complainer had been upstaged—by colleagues voicing his complaints with greater impact and coherence.

Frawley lost that second-round battle in Sydney, of course, but not before he had reproduced some of his Wimbledon form in pushing McEnroe to 7–5 in a hotly contested second set.

In the previous round, Frawley had beaten Peter Fleming, who was getting increasingly exasperated at his inability to overcome various nagging ailments so that he could start winning singles matches again. For a player who has tasted the thrill of being ranked in the world's top ten, seeing one's ranking slide uncontrollably toward the 100 mark is like being on the end of a parachute that hasn't opened. The thrill of a free fall can quickly turn to terror, and terror for a tennis pro is not being able to win anymore.

Fleming's match with Frawley had been played early in the day's program, and Peter had spent much of the late afternoon and evening nursing a succession of beers in the locker room. Combined with some medication he had been taking for one of his injuries, the beer had produced unhappy results. By the time McEnroe's match had finished, Fleming was, to put it mildly, a whiter shade of pale.

It was interesting to watch McEnroe at the Hordern Pavilion that evening. The "Brat" who has been called immature, irresponsible and childlike, among many worse names, did nothing particularly praiseworthy. In essence he merely looked after a friend. But it was the manner in which he coped with a series of overlapping situations that was significant, given the fact that this essentially shy young man had been content to remain in Fleming's shadow off court during their early years on the tour. Suddenly, "Junior" proved himself well capable of taking charge when his friend was in need.

During the course of about an hour that evening this surprisingly self-assured twenty-two-year-old had regaled a locker room full of players, including Tom Gullikson, Tony Graham, Paul Kronk, his old Stanford teammate Matt Mitchell, and trainer Paul Denny with stories of life on the Stanford team, dashed outside to greet a small group of people from America who had dropped by to say hello, signed some autographs, organized the stringing of a couple of rackets to be ready in time for his next match, and finally made sure that a driver had one of the cars ready right at the entrance so that the unsteady Fleming would not have too far to walk.

"Hang on—just two minutes and I'll have it organized," McEnroe shouted through the throng, holding up two fingers for emphasis so that the ashen-faced figure leaning against the locker-room doorpost at the end of the corridor would be sure to understand. Two minutes later "Junior" escorted his buddy outside, now brushing aside autograph hunters, as he took on the role of big protector for his stricken partner.

A couple of nights later, there came an opportunity to view another side of the McEnroe character, hyped up and overflowing with unused energy after a straightforward quarterfinal victory over Tom Gullikson. Reading a local paper while waiting to leave the stadium, McEnroe was reminded of John Thirsk, an Australian journalist who acts as ghost-writer for John Newcombe's syndicated column as well as reporting numerous tournaments under his own by-line. The name triggered the memory of an incident that had occurred a few weeks before during the U.S. Open at Flushing Meadow. Much to McEnroe's embarrassment, the New York *Daily News* had run a story about a secret weekend that the tennis star had spent with a well-known model in Florida during the summer. There had been a cooling period between John and Stacy Margolin following her early departure from Wimbledon, and his reported brief fling had been more in the nature of an experiment than anything serious. But now Stacy was back with him, staying at his parents' house during the Open, as the pair attempted to pick up where they had left off.

Having successfully managed to keep the *Daily News* away from Stacy all morning, John had been still trying to figure out how to explain everything to his house guest when Thirsk barged in on an extremely delicate situation by walking up to Stacy at Flushing Meadow with the newspaper in his hand and showing her the article. In his own defense, Thirsk, who had known John and Stacy for some time, maintained that he was simply trying to warn Stacy that all kinds of gossip columnists would be after her for quotes and reactions to the story. At best, Thirsk's action could be called thoughtless, but, of course, McEnroe's interpretation was a great deal less generous. He was already bristling over criticism leveled at him on CBS television by John Newcombe following their famous five-set doubles semifinal at the U.S. Open, and now the combination of that and what he considered the outrageous interference in his private life by Newk's ghost-writer produced a fairly predictable reaction.

"Where is that bastard Thirsk?" McEnroe demanded as he prepared to leave the locker room. "He keeps on telling me what a good friend

Racing for a wide ball from Vitas Gerulaitis in the semifinal of the 1981 U.S. Open, McEnroe falls backward into a courtside box, which just happens to be occupied by Stacy Margolin and big buddy Peter Rennert. *Popperfoto*

he is and then he does this sort of thing. You know it's not in my character to forgive and forget—not when someone fucks me over that badly. I'm going to tell him exactly what I think of him."

And that was precisely what he did. Ambushed by an enraged McEnroe as he passed the entrance to the locker-room area, Thirsk was abused in front of several startled people in the foulest language the New Yorker could summon up. There were messages for Newcombe, too, that were equally blunt, as McEnroe got it all off his chest, as if he were lancing some particularly unpleasant boil. Thirsk could do little except stand there and look hurt as McEnroe fired off a few more expletives and swept out into the rainy night.

Not a pleasant scene, nor one that did McEnroe's reputation any good. But at moments like that he is not concerned about his reputation. The righteous indignation that wells up inside him, fueled by all that burning nervous energy and wild Irish temper, thrusts the consequences of his actions aside as he zeroes in on his target. It is very rare that it erupts in this manner outside the tennis court and equally rare that it erupts without good cause. But the explosion when it comes tends to be terrifying and simply too vituperative for people to comprehend or tolerate.

McEnroe had no problem about channeling that energy in a more productive direction on the day of his Custom Credit semifinal against Eliot Teltscher. A big match and a worthy opponent are quite enough to concentrate his mind fiercely and compulsively on the task in hand. And for McEnroe there are few more worthy opponents than this wiry, gutsy little player who flails at the ball with such whirlwind speed that one is always afraid an arm might suddenly fly off into the stands. Quite apart from all the close matches they had played over the years, Eliot was on a hot streak, having taken McEnroe's TransAmerica title in San Francisco before making it to the final of the Mazda.

So, on a medium-paced indoor carpet that suited both players (after San Francisco, Teltscher had finally convinced himself he could play indoors), and with heavy Slazenger balls that enabled Eliot to pummel away with his sledgehammer ground strokes, the stage was set for a major battle. In fact it nearly turned into a war, both in the ferocity of the shotmaking, which boomed like cannon fire around the packed area, and in the intensity of the competition, which grated on both players' inflammable tempers. The match simmered, spluttered and frequently boiled over throughout two hours of extraordinary tennis.

McEnroe's incredible ability to take the power out of a shot and make the ball dance to his own tune—even a heavy ball that seemed lifeless to all the other players—was never more in evidence as Teltscher pounded away, belting forehands and backhands with equal velocity, while McEnroe clung desperately to a serve that was frequently under siege. Fourteen times Teltscher reached breakpoint on the champion's delivery, but the vital breakthrough was always denied him as McEnroe mixed up his serves into the ad court with cunning skill.

Nevertheless the struggle for the eleventh game of the second set, when the score stood at 5–5 with McEnroe having taken the first 7–5, was closer than anything that had gone before. Four times in that game Eliot came within one point of the break that would have left him serving for the set, but his opponent kept on coming up with those spellbinding touches of genius that separate the quick from the dead in contests of this caliber. Once, when Teltscher punched a cross-court forehand with such power that the ball must have been traveling at 90 mph or more when it crossed the net, McEnroe glided in to meet it with that loose and malleable wrist, turning the fizzing missile into a gentle drop volley that floated sweetly into a section of the forecourt

Eliot Teltscher, old-time McEnroe rival from their junior days, and now the eighth-ranked player in the world.
Richard Evans

that Eliot had no hope of reaching. In the players' box, where such skill is properly appreciated, the shot was greeted with a collective gasp of disbelief.

Dick Crealy, the veteran Australian touring pro who had been a popular figure—all six feet five inches of him—on the circuit throughout the seventies before retiring to take himself back to university, was standing open-mouthed at the back of the players' box for most of the match. "Jesus, if this is the way they hit the ball these days, I think I retired just in time!" Crealy chortled.

But, of course, it was not just the level of skill that made it so compelling. With McEnroe, there is always a lot more going on out there than pure shotmaking, especially when he is pitted against a player as intense as Teltscher. He was as wound up as I had seen him for many weeks, and naturally little in his own play met with his approval.

"Your ground strokes are putrid!" he yelled after hitting a backhand into the net. And then, when he just failed to reach a power-packed Teltscher forehand after sprinting across court with a burst of speed that would have left most athletes for dead, he cried out, "You're a fat hippopotamus!"—a comparison which, had they heard it, would have left hippos preening themselves with pride in mud pools all over Africa.

There were, of course, less amusing outbursts. The umpire was ridiculed for getting the score wrong, linesmen were yelled at, and numerous calls queried. Teltscher finally became convinced that for the first time in their long rivalry, McEnroe was milking the situation as a sly time-wasting ploy to upset his rhythm. Eliot had always succeeded in turning a deaf ear to the New Yorker's long-drawn-out battles with officialdom. But this time he became visibly upset at some of McEnroe's more elaborately staged complaints.

It was, nonetheless, high-octane entertainment, and the crowd, gulping its pre-popped beer, was enthralled. Upstairs, in a box reserved for Australia's pithy and expert tennis press, editors were calling for more copy as late editions went to bed. Richard Yallop, a "Pom" transplanted from *The Guardian* to the Melbourne *Age,* together with Mike Hurst of the Sydney *Telegraph* and Alan Clarkson of the Sydney *Morning Herald,* held McEnroe's attention at lengthy post-match press conferences with the probing intelligence of their questions. By and large, the Aussie press corps admired John for his honesty and appreciated him because he gave them good copy.

"Bugger whether or not you agree with everything he says or dislike what he does on court," said the veteran Clarkson, who has seen them all come and go in the sporting sphere over the past few years. "This kid is the best value in press conference you're likely to find today. He'll sit there, answer your questions seriously and tell you what he thinks. You can't ask more than that."

Predictably Doug Mason and Bill Bowrey, the former touring pro, got a different reaction from McEnroe when they asked him to wait on court after his matches so that they could ask him a few questions for Channel 10 television questions that would also be piped through the public address system at the Hordern Pavilion so that the crowd could listen in. "I'd rather not if that's all right," said McEnroe with a distinct tone of finality in his voice. "I don't want to make a big deal of this, but I really feel uncomfortable talking about the match immediately it's over with the crowd listening in."

Although Mason felt McEnroe was behaving like a prima donna, there is a difference for an innately shy person between talking in front of a crowd—and quite often a hostile crowd—and speaking to a group of reporters, most of whom are familiar, after a few precious moments to change shirts, cool down and collect one's thoughts.

As I recall, McEnroe relented toward the end of the week and Mason got his interview on court, but it was in press conference that McEnroe was at his most informative and interesting. He did his best, once again, to explain the tension that had surrounded his match with Teltscher after he had finally subdued the gallant Californian 7–5, 7–6, helping himself to a 7 points to 2 triumph in the second-set tie-break with a superb backhand pass down the line:

"Apart from the long rivalry we have had over the years, I really wanted to win because I do not want to suffer a letdown toward the end of the year. I don't want people saying, 'Oh, he might have won Wimbledon and the U.S. Open, but he can't maintain that kind of form.' That's why I am so nervous early on in Grand Prix tournaments. I can't afford to lose in the first or second round if I am to maintain my reputation as being the No. 1 player in the world. Once you get to the final the pressure eases because no one can say you had a bad week if you got to the final. I'll be more relaxed against Roscoe Tanner tomorrow, you'll see."

And he was. Despite the mental fatigue that had played its part in the various outbursts that had punctuated his play throughout the week, McEnroe slowly tightened his grip on Tanner during the course of a best-of-five-set final and retained his Custom Credit Indoor title in a good, calmly fought and generally uneventful match, 6–4, 7–5, 6–2.

With the major obstacle out of his way (for McEnroe, Teltscher tends to pose a bigger threat than Tanner), it had been time for a little relaxation the previous night. The Cauldron had become the most convenient and pleasant watering hole, with its proximity to the Hyatt and an obliging chef who kept churning out excellent steaks for hungry tennis players long after most restaurants had closed. After Teltscher and I had enjoyed a good dinner just before midnight, Eliot, not a man to dance the night away, went off to bed and I walked through to the bar area to finish off a glass of wine with John and Peter Fleming. McEnroe, attired in his usual faded blue coveralls, sat fidgeting with a beer as he tried to wind down from the high-pitched exertions of the match.

In the Australian spring of 1981, The Cauldron was definitely one of the livelier and more fashionable night spots in Sydney, and that, of course, meant that it attracted an above-average share of the city's best-looking girls. They noticed McEnroe, and McEnroe noticed them as they moved self-consciously past his table on the way to the dance floor.

Fleming's shy, sexy smile provided another reason for many to find an excuse to stop and chat, but the blond giant from New Jersey was not up for much else. Peter has never been the type to chase a different girl every night, and now that he was in love with Jenny Hudson, an English model whom he had met in London, he was quite content to spend the weeks away from her in the role of passive observer of whatever action the freewheeling tour bachelors like Vitas Gerulaitis, Peter Rennert, Tony Graham and Chris Dunk were drumming up.

Normally that would also have been true of McEnroe. But he was tiring of the long absences from Stacy and still wasn't quite sure how to handle them. The odd fling here and there gave him no particular satisfaction. It was all becoming too easy and too predictable as the availability of girls grew in direct proportion to his rise in fame and notoriety. But for McEnroe, the seeker of perfection, it was not quantity he was searching for but quality. And that, inevitably, led to frustration.

After watching another blond and beautiful example of Australian womanhood slink by, John shook his head and muttered, "If Stacy loves me, she ought to travel with me a bit more. This way is no good, man."

A few minutes later a couple of girls came over and started telling him how they had enjoyed his matches. One draped her arms around his neck from behind and made eyes at Peter across the table, while the other, standing to the side, eventually squatted down beside McEnroe so that she was gazing straight up into those clear blue eyes. His reaction was understandable. A tall brunette dressed in tight black jeans and top that outlined a perfect figure, the girl possessed that special allure which has more to do with feminine magnetism than classic beauty. She radiated appeal in a fresh, striking way that would have triggered a reaction in any half-alive heterosexual male. As the other girl moved off, she locked John in her gaze for several minutes as the pair of them conducted one of those hurried, breathless conversations that are heavy with innuendo. Eventually someone called her away, and McEnroe's eyes opened wide as he banged his beer mug on the table.

"Did you see *that,* man? She's just awesome!"

"She's also got a boy friend," said Fleming in an attempt to keep his partner in touch with reality.

"I'm not surprised," replied McEnroe. "And if I were him I wouldn't be far away."

He wasn't. A little while later the girl came back to whisper something in John's ear, but almost instantly she was yelled at by a tall, fierce-looking Aussie with a black moustache who obviously didn't take kindly to the thought of losing his bird to a famous twenty-two-year-old millionaire.

McEnroe was still mumbling words like "awesome" when the attractive blond waitress, who had been serving them drinks ever since they arrived, stopped by to ask if everything was all right. "No. Bring us some more beer and then don't go away. We need you," said McEnroe, exaggerating but not entirely faking his mood of loneliness and frustration.

Ros Wason, for that was the waitress's name, took it all in good part, having heard similar tales of woe many times before. And this time, of course, there was the unusual attraction of the famous face behind the plea for solace and comfort. As a model who was earning extra money in the time-honored manner, Ros could hold her own in looks with any of the girls gyrating on the nearby dance floor, and it was soon evident that she had enough humor and amusing conversation to interest McEnroe's impatient mind.

Later on, as the place was about to close, the reigning Wimbledon champion was to be found in The Cauldron's kitchen, looking a little like the hired help as he chatted with Ros, fiddled with a Sony Walkman and helped her clear the empty glasses from her tray. Away from the crowds, the stares and the giggling interlopers, John was much more relaxed and content. Yet they still made something of an incongruous pair, the waitress and the superstar, laughing and talking like old friends over the sink of a restaurant's kitchen at two in the morning. It is just possible that someone could have passed off the curly-haired young man in faded coveralls as one of the staff, but there is something about John McEnroe now, something about his look and his manner, that precludes confusion with a dishwasher, no matter how he is dressed or where he is found.

The next day, following his victory over Tanner, McEnroe was back in a familiar spotlight, answering Alan Clarkson's questions about how he had enjoyed his third visit to Australia. Blinded a little by the unusual warmth of the reception he received on his first trip, McEnroe had immediately pronounced it the country where he would most like to live after America. Now he was a little more critical. Certain aspects of the Australian psyche had been far too obvious to escape his notice.

"Everybody seems so uptight about whether or not something is true-blue Aussie or whatever you call it," he said. "The papers always go on about an *Aussie* runner breaking a record or an *Aussie* rider winning a race. It seems that we're a bit more relaxed about that sort of thing in America. But that's just one example. This trip I've come to realize we are really very different people, the Americans and Australians."

Not necessarily very diplomatic, not really what the Australian press wanted to hear, but pure McEnroe nonetheless—honest to the last, saying exactly what he thought, no matter if it cost him a little popularity. But the Aussies are big enough to take criticism. In fact, I often get the impression they are a little masochistic, and anyway they like a man who is not afraid to speak his mind.

13

TOKYO

The invitation from Mr. Masumi Esaki, chairman of the Seiko World Super Tennis Committee, was for cocktails and buffet in the Eminence Hall of the Keio Plaza Inter-Continental Hotel at 7:30 P.M. By the time Björn and Mariana Borg arrived, some twenty minutes later, the large banquet room in the hotel's South Tower was festooned with enough food to feed an army of Sumo wrestlers. Tennis players eat almost as much, however, and the thirty or so that were present went to work on the tempura stall and the mounds of other delicacies piled high in the middle of the room with a vengeance.

Of course, thirty tennis players and a few wives don't fill a room that size, but Seiko executives and associates do. As usual in Japan, companies never fall short of producing guests to round out an occasion such as this, and as the Seiko World Tennis event—now the richest indoor tournament on the Volvo Grand Prix tour—was employing no less than two thousand people to make sure it worked like . . . well, like a Seiko, there were more than enough bodies present to fill Eminence Hall. Not to mention the photographers.

A battery of flashbulbs had popped as Borg arrived, but when John McEnroe walked in a few minutes later, I thought the Japanese were staging their version of July 4. There must have been at least thirty photographers blinding everyone within range as they clicked away, jostling around McEnroe as he tried to move across the room.

Over in a corner by one of the little food stalls that were being manned by enthusiastic Japanese cooks, Buster Mottram was observing the scene with a typically inquiring eye. "It's amazing how quickly things change," he commented. "There's Borg, a guy who has won five Wimbledons, and he's practically being ignored here tonight. Yet they are falling over McEnroe."

"That's the way the world is," retorted Paul McNamee, ever the realist, as he munched on a leg of teriyaki chicken.

An anguished face stares out from a magazine cover as Balazs Taroczy's wife, Bori, ATP trainer Dave Fechtman (*center*), and Eliot Teltscher enjoy the Tokyo sunshine during the Japan Open. *Richard Evans*

Shaking hands over a keg of sake in Tokyo for the first time since McEnroe assumed the mantle of the world's No. 1 player by beating Borg at the U.S. Open two months earlier. *Dentsu Agency, Tokyo*

In fact, I think Buster was guilty of a little exaggeration, although he did have a point. Borg had received his fair share of attention as he and Mariana stood chatting with Rosemary and Tim Gullikson, but there was no doubt that McEnroe was the hot number as far as the press was concerned. When I took Hong Kong tournament director Ken Catton over to meet McEnroe, we were immediately dazzled by the popping of flashbulbs. As usual John was not comfortable in the artificial spotlight. "If they don't stop soon, I'm getting out of here," he mumbled in my ear. "There are so many of them!"

In fact McEnroe stuck it out with relatively good humor and obliged the Seiko publicity office to the extent of shaking Borg's hand (for the first time, incidentally, since he did so across the net in Flushing Meadow) and breaking open a wooden casket of sake in a traditional ceremony with his arch-rival while the insatiable photographers clicked their way through a few more rolls of film.

There was to be more evidence of McEnroe's soaring worldwide fame as the week wore on—a week, by the way, which produced some of the most surprising results I had ever witnessed on the pro tour, as well as a surprising attack by McEnroe on a fellow player. But it all started quietly enough, with McEnroe easing his way past John Sadri in a match that was a pale shadow of their great NCAA final three years before. After a brief stopover in Honolulu to play some golf with Peter Fleming, McEnroe had arrived in Tokyo early enough to accustom himself to the incredibly fast Supreme court that had been laid on boards covering the ice rink at the vast Olympic Gymnasium. Although McEnroe enjoys fast surfaces—they suit him temperamentally as well as technically—he was the first to admit that this one was too fast for good spectator tennis. Under the circumstances, Sadri might have been expected to give the No. 1 seed some trouble with a serve that has been rated as one of the most dangerous in the game in recent years. But Sadri was having trouble with his timing and rhythm on a delivery that was beginning to look a little muscle bound, and he went down, 6–2, 6–2.

Tsuyoshi Fukui, Japan's No. 1 ranked player, went one game better against McEnroe in the second round, proving himself a quick and agile net player as he parried some of the American's best returns during the course of an entertaining 6–3, 6–2 defeat that drew the occasional sigh of appreciation from a critical audience. McEnroe had to work hard at times but apparently still needed the fix of a verbal blast at someone to get the adrenaline pumping.

After demanding that a television cameraman be moved right at the beginning of the match, McEnroe soon turned his attention to the umpire. When the Japanese official refused to reply to his query over a

Björn Borg, with Mariana at his side, appears almost openmouthed at the sagacity of the author at the Seiko party in Tokyo in November 1981. *Dentsu Agency, Tokyo*

line call, McEnroe looked over at Bill Gilmour, the Sydney referee who was acting as Grand Prix supervisor at the Seiko, and called out sarcastically, "An umpire who doesn't speak English, Supervisor? Good choice."

That was just the opening skirmish in a series of confrontations that was to build into a mighty conflagration before the week was out. Even in this match McEnroe was not finished with Gilmour, a pleasant, experienced official who had started his tennis career, auspiciously enough, as Lew Hoad's doubles partner in junior tournaments before Lew found himself a little fellow called Ken Rosewall to play with. At the beginning of the second set, McEnroe queried another dubious call and, after getting no satisfaction from the umpire, rounded angrily on Gilmour.

"You ought to be ashamed of yourself," he shouted. "Call yourself a former player? You never do anything for the players!"

Sitting next to me in the players' enclosure, Pat Dupré's lovely wife Darcy shook her head in amazement. "What's he doing that for?" she asked. "It looks so bad and it's so unnecessary." Darcy was, of course, merely echoing the sentiments of millions who had watched this ugly ritual enacted in tennis arenas all over the world.

I have quoted McEnroe verbatim so it can be seen that no swear words were used. By cutting out obscenity on all but the rarest occasions, John often escapes censure from officials who are slightly intimidated by him and would prefer to find an excuse to do nothing rather than force a showdown in the middle of a match. This, however, does not always mean that they refrain from fining him later, which, in my opinion, is something of the coward's way out. I think Gilmour was guilty of this kind of reaction in this instance, for he let the incident pass.

It is all a question of when to stamp down on McEnroe and when to allow him a little license to let off some of the steam that builds like a pressure cooker inside him. Kurt Nielsen, the Dane who twice reached the Wimbledon singles final in the fifties and is the only other Grand Prix supervisor with top-class playing experience, understands the way to handle McEnroe better than most.

"There is no point in picking on John for the small things like hitting a ball into the net in frustration," Nielsen told me when we discussed the problem during the Bangkok Tennis Classic a few weeks later. "That only makes him mad and he retaliates, which, in some circumstances, I can understand. You should always wait until he does something really bad—something *he* knows is out of line. If you have been fair and reasonable with him up to then, he will react pretty well to admonishment. You will see the head go down in embarrassment as he realizes he has gone too far. But it is a fine dividing line for an umpire or a supervisor to detect and act upon in the heat of the moment."

The dividing line for leniency stops, in my opinion, the moment a player starts telling an official in public that he ought to be ashamed of himself. It is simply not the player's place to make that kind of comment. If Gilmour had made it plain he would not tolerate insolence right at the beginning, he might possibly have avoided the explosion that ultimately altered the whole outcome of the tournament.

On Wednesday night John invited me over to the Okura, generally considered one of the top two or three hotels in a city that rightly prides itself on the quality of accommodations that it offers visitors. McEnroe and Borg were both staying there so that they would be spared some of the constant attention everyone was receiving at the Keio Plaza.

As we walked through the crowded lobby of one of the world's most cosmopolitan hotels, I realized just how much McEnroe needed all the privacy he could get. Nine people out of ten that we passed on our way to the Okura's magnificent Chinese restaurant either commented on McEnroe to the people they were with or gave some other indication of knowing who he was. Four times during dinner groups of businessmen of various nationalities—American, Japanese, British and Norwegian among them—came over and interrupted our conversation. They wanted autographs, and only one bothered to trot out the normal excuse about it being for his daughter. Yet they were all from that middle-class, over-thirty-five age group that is supposed to object so strongly to McEnroe's attitude and behavior.

They got their autographs but little else. All attempts to engage John in small talk failed. He doesn't like small talk with strangers, especially when they are interrupting his meal. But like so much else about him, his monosyllabic replies provided a very deceptive indication of his ability to express himself. By the time we had finished with the almond chicken and sweet-and-sour pork, John was in full flow, making his points with such vehemence that heads started turning at nearby tables. Attracted by the pitch of his voice and that special kind of electricity that he seems to give off in crowded places, people wanted to find out who he was—this young American with his jacket slung casually across the back of his chair. After one glance few had to be told.

We covered a whole range of subjects and human emotions, for there is little that goes on in the world that escapes McEnroe's attention, although, by his own admission, he is still ignorant about the finer points of much of what he sees and reads. After the third or fourth interruption for an autograph, we got onto the subject of fame and its liabilities.

"You know, I don't enjoy what goes with it," McEnroe said. "I mean, it's nice to be recognized and to come to a nice place like this and have no trouble getting a table or whatever. But mostly it's a pain when you can't even walk around without people bothering you. I was watching Prince Charles and Princess Diana on television this evening. They were on a tour of Wales or something. I really feel for that girl. All day she has to smile and go through all that bullshit. And she's only twenty—younger than me. That's going to be her whole life. But she does it pretty well, I must say."

It has taken a long time—a peculiarly long time for such a quick learner—for McEnroe to come to terms with the fact that, as a top-class public performer elevated to superstar status, he cannot be a celebrity only when he is performing and then revert to a private person the moment he walks away from the arena. The public—yes, those same people whose avid interest in what one does makes one rich—are insatiable. They want great chunks of their idol and feed off every tidbit voraciously. The press always gets it in the neck, but in fact the popular newspapers are "popular" precisely because they are providing what the public craves.

Sammy Davis, Jr., who admittedly was something of an extremist on the subject, always used to tell me he "owed" the public every time he stepped out of his front door. "They made me and they have a right to my time," Sammy used to say in those high-flying days when he would invite about thirty people to the White Elephant in Curzon Street every night during his London shows. Few entertainers would share Davis' enthusiasm for public contact, and certainly McEnroe, now as big a celebrity as Sammy ever was, views it very differently, despite the fact that he very, very rarely refuses any reasonable request for an autograph. However, he is genuinely disgusted by the continual probing and dissecting of celebrities' private lives and private problems.

"Did you see that show Dan Rather did on Elvis Presley the other day?" McEnroe went on. "I mean, Rather's a good reporter or whatever, but he started coming up with all sorts of fatuous theories about why Elvis was into drugs and all that shit. It doesn't need any heavy theories, man. He was into drugs because of what the world did to him. And anyway it's none of anybody's God-damn business. And that goes for politicians, too, as far as I am concerned. If a congressman likes bananas up his ass, so what! As long as he does his job properly it's got nothing to do with anybody else."

McEnroe's voice was rising in concert with his strength of feeling on the subject, and I thought I detected a slight lull in the conversation at an adjacent table during that little discourse. There is no doubt that he does feel strongly about the indignities that so-called stars are put through by their fans and the press; and although he would do well to take heed of something *Time* magazine media columnist Thomas Griffith wrote recently, "Only the inexperienced can expect a journalistic transaction to be risk free," McEnroe can honestly maintain that he doesn't want anything to do with journalistic transactions in the first place. He has turned down enough money thrust at him by eager editors all over the world—especially in Britain—to look anyone in the eye on that score.

But he is, or until very recently has been, inexperienced in the whole area of relations with the media, and even if he can never bring himself to enjoy what Griffith describes as "check-out counter celebrity journalism," he must, for the sake of his own sanity if nothing else, learn to live with it. The actor Richard Harris, with more than twenty-five years experience in the spotlight over McEnroe, has learned to be thoroughly philosophical about it all. "John should realize there is nothing you can do to stop the press printing lies about you. They do it all the time," Harris told me one day when we were discussing

McEnroe's problem. "There are good reporters and bad ones, and you've just got to learn to take it all as it comes. Of course, it annoys you initially, but now I refuse to worry about it. Every time some huge load of garbage is written about me I just think about how much more I'm going to up my fees next time my agent calls. Right or wrong, your price goes up every time your name hits the headlines. People pay to see someone they read about all the time."

It will take McEnroe a little while yet to reach that happy state of mind, but if Harris, one of the original wild Irishmen, can have achieved it, there is hope for anyone. It is easy to forget how young McEnroe still is and how little he has experienced in many areas of life, for he seems to have been in the headlines for so long. He started to tell me about Irish traditions regarding the funeral of a family member and remarked that he had only been to one funeral, and even that was not for a member of his own family:

"It was just after I had lost to Connors in five sets in the final of Philadelphia in 1980. One of my father's best friends had just died, and I flew back to New York to go to the funeral with my parents. For once in my life I was glad I hadn't won. Everything was so bad that day that I felt it was better I was feeling bad, too. It would have seemed so totally inappropriate if I had come home with something to be happy about.

"It's the Irish tradition that everyone goes back to the deceased's house after the funeral for some kind of a party to try and cheer everyone up. But, of course, after a few drinks the women started crying, and then, on this occasion, a fifty-year-old guy broke down and started sobbing. God, it was awful. I'm just so lucky my parents are so young. They're both forty-six and I'll be twenty-three next year. I've been really lucky being spared any real tragedies in my immediate family. It's so hard to conceive. The worst shock I ever had was when I phoned up Stacy as soon as I got back from Wimbledon in 1977 after getting to the semis unseeded. I hadn't spoken to her for a few days while I had been over in England, and I was excited about how well I'd done and was all ready to tell her and she goes, 'My father just died.' I was so stunned, man. I just didn't know what to say. I mean, I felt such an idiot being all happy about doing well at Wimbledon and there she is burying her father in Los Angeles."

After we had run the gauntlet of gaping diners and escaped back upstairs, we continued talking in John's room for a while, whenever the phone was not ringing. First it was Mel Purcell, just checking out the night's action before he hit the town, and then McEnroe's Japanese interpreter called with all sorts of suggestions as to how John might like to spend the remaining hours of the evening.

"He's a really nice guy who's just trying to make sure I have a good time," John said. "He's always wanting to do something for me, but he doesn't seem to realize there is nothing much I want to do before I play. I mean, if I went anywhere it would have to be in the car and it would all be a big deal. I can't exactly stroll around out there by myself, can I?"

On the evidence of what I had witnessed on our short journeys to and from the restaurant, that much was certainly true. So I left him, lying on his bed, watching closed-circuit television amidst the usual litter of clothes, rackets, cassette tapes and dirty socks that decorate most tennis players' hotel rooms—his wasn't as chaotic as Nastase's used to be, but it was close—and took the sort of stroll through the nearby nightclub district of Roppongi that is no longer a feasible form of relaxation for a twenty-two-year-old tennis pro as famous as John McEnroe. Such is the price of success.

McEnroe was taking particular care over his beauty sleep that night. Earlier than he might have expected, considering how long some players go without being drawn against each other on the circuit, the draw in the Seiko had given him an opportunity to exact revenge on Bill Scanlon, the talented Texan who had beaten him in San Francisco four weeks before. McEnroe and Scanlon were old rivals but not good friends. Although they were both passionately into modern music, they found each other insufferable on court, and this precluded any hope of building a friendship out of common interests.

Scanlon is a strange young man. Amusing, likable, imaginative and unorthodox by the standards of the programmed modern-day tennis pro, "Scaz," as his friends call him, is the sort of person who, on winning a Grand Prix title on the Hawaiian island of Maui a few years before, promptly quit the tour and stayed there for several weeks, spending his prize money and playing the guitar under the Pacific stars with Dickie Dell—brother of super-agent Donald—and assorted female friends.

On court Scanlon strums a different tune. Considerably more serious about his career now, Bill is considered a "niggling" opponent by many players on the tour. He appears to adopt a supercilious attitude that includes barely detectable time-wasting tactics and surreptitious comments to the umpire about his opponent's behavior. This last habit, in particular, is what drives McEnroe mad. As soon as John queries a call, Bill is likely to tell the umpire not to be intimidated. Some players, who feel that McEnroe does earn himself the benefit of the doubt too often by his constant bitching, would applaud this action. However, it does flout the unwritten law most players, including more often than not McEnroe himself, adhere to, which says that a player should stay the hell out of any dispute between his opponent and an official.

San Francisco had not been the first time that there had been trouble between the two of them, and this time McEnroe was determined not merely to win but to teach Scanlon a lesson. I had never seen him actively and deliberately go after another player before, although there had, of course, been numerous on-court arguments which had sprung up spontaneously during the course of a match—especially in doubles. However, it eventually became apparent that there was nothing spontaneous about this calculated snub.

The first outburst came in the tenth game of the first set with McEnroe leading 5–4 on serve. The umpire overruled a linesman's call in McEnroe's favor, and Scanlon immediately started talking to the official in confidential tones. That was enough for the New Yorker. "You're lower than dirt," he shouted angrily at Scanlon. Bill's reaction was to run up to the umpire again and be rewarded when McEnroe was given a conduct warning for "abuse of an opponent." However, the incident had obviously affected Scanlon because he double-faulted the set away and never really threatened to halt McEnroe's grim-faced

Phone calls while away another night in a hotel room—this time the opulent Okura in Tokyo. *Richard Evans*

march to victory by 6–4, 6–3. It was then that McEnroe made his most dramatic gesture. As Scanlon came up to the net to shake hands, McEnroe pointedly walked away toward his chair, picked up his rackets and left his opponent standing there with his hand held out, looking a bit foolish. Six thousand Japanese, stunned at this breach of etiquette, sat in silence for a few seconds and then loudly applauded Scanlon as he left the court.

With only trainer Dave Fechtman in attendance, there was no way the pair could avoid each other in the small locker room, and anyway McEnroe was quite content to make the final point. "Now maybe you'll understand what it's like playing you, Scanlon. I just gave you some of your own medicine, that's all."

"Well fuck you, too," retorted Scanlon, whose customary command of the English language seemed to have deserted him temporarily.

Perhaps the most interesting aspect of the whole sorry affair was McEnroe's refusal to explain himself publicly when asked about the incidents in the press conference. In a bid to cut off the inquiries on the subject immediately, John told the charming and quick-witted interpreter Mimi Yoshii to tell everyone that it was a private matter and that he was not prepared to discuss it.

This reaction provided another classic example of just how hard and uncompromising McEnroe can be, even to his own detriment. It was obvious he had come off as the villain of the piece as far as the public and press were concerned, for no one in Japan knew of any prior antipathy between the two men; and on the face of it, McEnroe had simply made Scanlon look a fool for no reason. But even though he knew full well that Scanlon could follow him into the press conference and say anything he liked (in fact Bill did not appear at all), McEnroe was quite prepared to let people come to whatever conclusions they wished. As far as he was concerned, it was a matter for Scanlon and himself, and if it left him with egg on his face, too bad.

Later, McEnroe opened up and explained his feelings to me: "I told him he was too good a player to get up to those tricks. He's beaten me twice in about eight meetings, and he can do so fair and square. But he's always trying to get through the umpire by saying things behind my back which no one else hears. He tries to make out I'm the only one who argues over line calls. Well, this time I wasn't going to stand for it and I really lost my cool. I've never wanted to win a match by upsetting my opponent before, but I did this time. Did you see how he double-faulted on set point? I'm not sorry. He had it coming to him."

McEnroe had something coming to him as well, in the form of another fine. Unfortunately, in light of what transpired, supervisor Bill Gilmour failed to reach McEnroe to notify him of the fine before he left the stadium that night. So, as Grand Prix rules state that players must be informed of any fines levied against them very soon after the decision has been made, Gilmour had no option but to hand John the fine when he turned up next day for his semifinal match against Vince Van Patten. It would have been bad timing under any circumstances, but given the sensitivity of the whole situation and the nature of the fine—"abuse of an opponent," which was an unusual one for John—it was tantamount to striking matches too near the gasoline tank. What finally set the whole thing ablaze was the revelation that McEnroe was the only player to have been fined by Gilmour. For John, that was the final straw. He and several other people had heard one of the Americans call a linesman "a bloody little Nip," and Scanlon himself had stuck up a middle finger at McEnroe at the end of the match—a gesture that has cost Nastase thousands of dollars in fines over the years. Yet Gilmour had taken no notice of any of that. Once again McEnroe was being singled out as the lone culprit. It was that which made McEnroe see red of a brighter hue than even he was used to.

People within earshot—and they did not have to stand too close—said it was a memorable performance, not merely for the screaming intensity of the invective that poured out of the player's mouth but for the length of time he sustained it. "I called him every name in the book," McEnroe admitted later. "I went berserk. I was really mad. I must have yelled at him for a good ten minutes."

The unfortunate Gilmour was appalled at the level of emotional hysteria that McEnroe's temper reached. For a moment he seemed to be on the point of delirium. Again one wondered how so much electric energy could pour out of one body. But, of course, once the storm had passed, there was nothing left. Due on court fifteen minutes later, John soon found he couldn't hit a ball. He double-faulted on the first point and Van Patten was a set and 3–0 up with a point for a double break before McEnroe could offer more than token resistance.

The row with Gilmour was not made public at the time, but there is no doubt in my mind that it was the prime cause of his loss to Van Patten. I am loath to detract from the finest victory in Vinnie's career, but the fact remains that McEnroe is one of those high-stress performers who need to conserve all their energy for the battle ahead.

In this respect McEnroe is just like Connors, who never even wants to watch a movie on television prior to a match for fear that it will get his adrenaline pumping too early and so lower his level of tension before he gets on court. Both these highly strung stars nurse their energy like broody hens about to hatch an egg. This time, of course, McEnroe had hatched too early and consequently was emotionally spent before the first ball was struck.

Against a less accomplished and less determined opponent than Van Patten, he might have been able to give the starter another kick late in the second set and save himself from defeat. But that week in Tokyo, Van Patten, the actor who had turned himself into a top-class tennis pro, was keeping a date with destiny. And if that sounds like a good line for a television soap opera, let me assure you Van Patten's exploits in the Seiko went beyond the bounds of plausibility as far as any Hollywood script is concerned. Rarely have I seen fact make such a strong bid to live up to its reputation for being stranger than fiction.

Vinnie had had a lousy year. Sick from January until April, injured in August, and beaten in the first round of just about every tournament he played in between, Van Patten had entered the Seiko with his ATP ranking in danger of dipping below the 100 mark for the first time since he had joined the circuit full time three years before. But with his quick eye and high-steppin' dancer's feet, Van Patten found the ultra-fast surface in Tokyo ideal and quickly got into his stride by defeating the highly promising Australian John Fitzgerald, 6–2, 6–4. But that, as they say in L.A., was just for openers. In successive rounds the young man with red bandanna tied around his golden locks—for the sake of superstition, neither was washed all week—proceeded to take out the No. 5 seed Jose-Luis Clerc, the No. 12 seed Vitas Gerulaitis, and then McEnroe himself. Having cut that kind of a swath to the final, it was a tribute to Van Patten's icy determination and ability to grasp the opportunity he had created for himself that he didn't suffer a letdown at the final hurdle. That tough and experienced pro Mark Edmondson, enjoying the most consistently successful year of his career, was just the sort of player to knock off some will-o-the-wisp one-day wonder who is prancing along with his head in the clouds. But although Edo had a sequence of winning sixteen consecutive points on his own serve after Van Patten had won the first set, the actor improvised with a new script in the final set and came up with enough inventive stroke play off his double-fisted returns and lunging volleys to snatch the $55,000 first prize with a 6–2, 3–6, 6–3 victory.

At the moment of his first real triumph in tennis, Van Patten's theatrical upbringing did not desert him. Before accepting the trophy, he bowed solemnly to the crowd of eight thousand and then blew kisses to his Japanese fan club, which had been formed some years before when one of his television series was being shown in Tokyo. For Vinnie the week had turned into the kind of fairy tale every middle-ranked touring pro dreams about, and the amount of additional press coverage his success received mollified Seiko executives who were not very happy about the way the Grand Prix rules had been implemented over the McEnroe fine.

Gen Matsumoto, the shrewd businessman who, along with Eiichi Kawatei and former Japanese No. 1 Osamu Ishiguro, had been instrumental in building up the Japanese Professional Tennis Association, realized full well that McEnroe's defeat had been due, at least in part, to the fact that he had been handed his fine just before he went on court.

"We are not happy about that," Matsumoto told me as Van Patten, perfectly at ease in the spotlight, gave a gracious victory speech at a party held that night for the tournament staff at the Keio Plaza. "We do not think it was fair on the player or the tournament, because obviously we wanted the biggest drawing card to be playing in his best frame of mind. There has to be a better way to implement the rules."

Saigo, of the powerful Dentsu PR agency that was responsible for the tournament promotion, was particularly sensitive to the situation as Björn Borg, whom everyone had hoped and expected to see play McEnroe in the final, had fallen to Tim Gullikson in the second round. Certainly the situation could have been handled better—and the superefficient Seiko organization surely deserved to be better served by the Grand Prix rules than they were—but there was no denying the identity of the real culprit and, as usual, he didn't try to hide.

"It was my own stupid fault," McEnroe admitted to me once he had forced himself to sit through another press conference tactfully handled by the beautiful Mimi after the Van Patten match. "There was no way I should have allowed myself to get into a raging argument with Gilmour just before I went on court. I couldn't hit a ball for five games. But when I saw I was the only one to get fined I couldn't believe it. Was I the only one to see Scanlon stick his finger up at me? Gilmour says he never saw it. I was so mad I just screamed at him. But at least I started playing a little in the second set. That was better than if I had ended up losing three and love without ever getting started. Vinnie played well. He kept changing the pace on me which made it even more difficult to get a proper feel on the ball."

McEnroe was trying to sound matter-of-fact about it when in reality he was exhausted, annoyed and confused in almost equal parts.

"What am I going to do about these fines, man?" he asked me in a desperate tone as he waited to collect his prize money at the stadium before facing the long trek out to Narita Airport. "I'm only a few hundred dollars off the suspension limit, and you know I'll never manage to get through a week in London with a clean sheet. Not with those umpires."

After cursing at a photographer who kept lurking around wherever we were talking, McEnroe thought for a minute and then continued, "What happens about the Davis Cup if I get suspended after Wem-

Vincent Van Patten and interpreter, Mimi, facing the press after his victory in the Seiko Championship, November 1981. *Richard Evans*

bley? Do Grand Prix rules apply for the Davis Cup? Because that's all I care about right now. I can't afford to get suspended for the Davis Cup. Maybe I ought to bag London. I hate doing that but I really wonder whether it's the right place for me to go in my present state of mind."

He was thinking out loud, happy to have his thoughts fall on relatively sympathetic ears as the antagonism built up all around him. He looked tired and thoroughly dispirited. "I just feel I'm fighting the whole world," he said. "But it's the same old story. I get to a pitch where everything and everyone start bugging me and then I know I've done it again. I've played too much. God, I've said it so many times but I must cut down."

Of course, he did not run out on a commitment. He went to London and ultimately gave Len Owen and his Benson & Hedges Championships the most memorable final in the tournament's history. No doubt Owen thanked him for helping create more publicity than even a cigarette company could afford to buy, but mostly all he received was more abuse. I wasn't there but I know what he did. He was rude to people—some people, some of the time. It was hardly surprising.

Naturally his action against Scanlon was the talk of the Asian circuit for weeks afterward. He was breaking dangerous ground by humiliating a fellow player because it made them all feel threatened by someone they already considered quite dangerous enough as a legitimate opponent. His talent had set him apart, but until now he had always been perfectly approachable in the locker room where his shell seemed to dissolve slightly amidst such familiar surroundings. To a far greater degree than Borg, Vilas or some of the other top stars who had begun traveling with an entourage, McEnroe had remained one of the boys.

And again, until now, his outbursts had always been directed against the common enemy, officials, even if they did sometimes disturb the other man's concentration. But that was no longer quite true. Even if several players secretly applauded McEnroe for having had the guts to give Scanlon a lesson that he may have deserved, a communal feeling sprang up which was fueled by envy and fear. They now had an excuse to sling a few verbal darts at this tough, arrogant leader of their tight and desperately competitive little world.

As is so often the case, the wrong players led the attack. Hank Pfister, the big Californian who had had a run-in with McEnroe during a doubles match in Hawaii the year before, was the first to condemn the temporarily fallen champion. "He's got no reason to complain about anything," Pfister declared as the subject came up for heated discussion in the players' lounge the following day. "He ought to learn to behave himself."

I thought at the time that there was a little of the pot accusing the kettle syndrome about that remark, and ironically, as I write this far from the scene of the current action at the WCT World of Doubles in Birmingham, word reached me on the radio of a certain Mr. Pfister being fined for calling an umpire a cheat. But I doubt very much that it made the front page of the London *Daily Mirror* in the form of an editorial advising Hank to get the hell home to California. Lesser players like Pfister rarely have to endure such hysterical wrath.

The discussion was still going on over breakfast in the coffee shop of the Excelsior Hotel in Hong Kong the following week. Vince Van Patten, Tim and Rosemary Gullikson, Bruce Manson, Lloyd Bourne and Bill Scanlon himself were all engaged in what, by then, had become a favorite topic of conversation.

Needless to say, McEnroe supporters were rather thin on the ground, with Scanlon conducting the orchestra. But "Scaz" did manage to come up with a few comments that were tinged with a grudging admiration. "He's a good street fighter, I'll say that for him," said Scanlon. "He'll come up with a few comments that are a bit tough to counter. Do you remember what he said to Pfister when they had that row in the doubles in Maui last year?

"Mac said to Hank, 'Why are you getting so worked up about doubles? Is it because you can't win any singles matches anymore?' Jesus, I mean what can you say to *that?* And then there was that time he told Kriek, 'At least I say what I think of you to your face instead of having you read it in the newspapers next day.' You've got to hand it to the guy—he is direct!"

But probably not as popular with some of his peers as he had been. Friendship and popularity among a bunch of egocentric athletes, who are essentially out to beat each other into the ground, hang by a fragile thread at the best of times, and these days it takes less than it ever did for this to snap. In that respect the tennis circuit has changed enormously over the past ten years. Rivalries were great but friendships were real in the early days of open tennis. Now the money is too big and the pressure too intense. It is virtually a different world with different values.

Ironically, no one feels this more keenly than McEnroe himself. Although he is both an instigator and a victim of present-day dog-eat-dog mentality, I am sure he yearns for a greater sense of camaraderie amongst his peers. On more than one occasion, John has told me, "I never knew the circuit in the old days but I know it has changed. No one gives a shit about anyone else deep down. Everybody's just out for himself. It stinks."

But certain aspects of it never change. I was reminded of that when I was invited to the International Club of Japan's annual dinner at the Takanawa Prince Hotel during the Japan Open. I was fortunate enough to sit opposite the I.C. president, Yoshiro Ohta, now a venerable gentleman of eighty-one. Apart from making a speech in almost faultless English, over dinner Mr. Ohta took us back into other eras of the game and spoke with twinkling eyes of the time he played on the Centre Court at Wimbledon in 1927 and also of a Davis Cup match he played against the United States.

"I had to play Bill Tilden and I won the first set 7–5," Mr. Ohta recalled. "But then he changed the pace on me and I lost the next three sets rather quickly!"

The following week John McEnroe was caught out by Vince Van Patten's changes of pace—a similar complaint fifty years on. But in other respects it is a rather different game from the one they played in Mr. Ohta's time.

14

THE DAVIS CUP

There is nothing that confounds McEnroe's critics so totally as his unwavering dedication to the Davis Cup. Spoiled, selfish, greedy, a man alone who wants everything his own way—this is the portrait that McEnroe-haters try to sell, and some of it may, indeed, seem plausible until one analyzes his record in team competition. We have heard Stanford University coach Dick Gould on the subject. "The best team player I ever had," said Gould. Those sentiments are echoed by everyone who has been associated with him in Davis Cup play.

Roscoe Tanner, a player from an older generation who had never been particularly close to McEnroe prior to the 1981 Davis Cup campaign, quickly got a new insight into the man when he filled the No. 2 singles berth against Australia and Argentina. "I understand him a lot better now and have come to appreciate his special qualities," Tanner told me. "He is totally supportive and a really fine team man."

Even Arthur Ashe, the United States captain, who had serious disagreements with McEnroe on questions of conduct, has frequently praised John's dedication to the cause. "When the chips are down, John doesn't send his excuses—he's there!" Ashe wrote in his syndicated column.

Even Ashe cannot make the claim that he has never, ever turned down the chance to play Davis Cup for the United States. But McEnroe can. And in that he is alone among the present generation of American players. From the very first time he was selected, he played, no questions asked, no demands made, come rain or come shine. And it is not only Connors and various other American players who have discovered convenient excuses for sidestepping Davis Cup duty in recent years. For a variety of reasons, Borg has often turned his back on the Swedish Davis Cup team. Orantes and Higueras both retired early from service in Spanish colors. And, of course, it took quite a while before Britain's own Buster Mottram, now such a valiant Davis Cup competitor, would agree to play under the captaincy of Paul Hutchins.

There was no doubt that before ITF secretary David Gray pushed through legislation for a revised and streamlined Davis Cup format in 1981, the age-old competition did stick an anachronistic—not to say costly—cog in the free-spinning, free-earning wheel that carries the modern-day tennis star around the world's circuit. The Borgs, McEnroes and Connors can earn as much as $150,000—and considerably more under certain circumstances—for exhibition matches during the free weeks on the Grand Prix calendar. But Davis Cup, which is scheduled to fall into those free weeks, pays only about $200,000 to the winning *team* after four rounds. In the mega-buck language favored by Hollywood moguls, the superstars are playing Davis Cup for peanuts—several thousand dollars amounting to peanuts by their standards—and some just don't feel it is worth their while.

I don't necessarily blame them for that. I have never subscribed to the theory that it is one's duty to play for one's country just because its LTA gave a helping hand up the ladder (especially as it is often a pretty feeble helping hand in the first place). I have always considered blind patriotism far more dangerous than desirable. However, having said that, there is no way one can detract from the selfless service McEnroe has given the United States over the past four years. John and Kay McEnroe can properly take full credit for making selection for America's Davis Cup team the shining pinnacle of achievement in Junior's eyes. "John was brought up to believe playing for your country was the greatest possible honor," said his father. "There has never been a moment's hesitation about his being available to play and wanting to play."

The manufactured magnificence of the sprawling Mission Hills Country Club in Rancho Mirage, California, saw the honor bestowed on nineteen-year-old John McEnroe when he was picked to play singles for his country for the first time in the 1978 Davis Cup final against Britain. The report I wrote for *Tennis Week* bears a second look in the light of subsequent events:

With John McEnroe as point man and Stan Smith and Bob Lutz the lynchpin of their success, Tony Trabert's team brought the Davis Cup back to the United States for the first time since 1972 with a thoroughly convincing 4–1 defeat of Britain.

Yet in all probability, it will be British tennis that will benefit most from the year's campaign that ended on a strangely unreal note at the Mission Hills Country Club near Palm Springs.

It is unlikely that the average American sports fan will consider regaining the Davis Cup one of his country's major sporting achievements for 1978. To an outside observer it seems that America only really gets behind its athletes in a team sense once every four years at the Olympics. This may change when the United States finally produces a soccer team capable of challenging Argentina, Brazil or West Germany. Until then American sport will continue to live in its cozy, esoteric little world, pretending that the Los Angeles Dodgers playing the New York Yankees actually qualifies as a "World" Series.

In Britain, however, the achievements of team manager Paul Hutchins in taking his team to the finals against considerable odds should generate sufficient interest and pride to stimulate much-needed growth in the game.

It would have been stretching credibility a little far to have expected a better result against a team as powerful as that fielded by Trabert in the final. But some British visitors were disappointed by the somewhat contrived and artificial atmosphere in which the tie was played.

Given the time available to set up the final, I doubt if a better site could be found. It was technically and aesthetically correct for the U.S. to want to play outdoors and that, considering the December date, inevitably restricted one's options.

I think the problem lies in the image so many of us have of the correct setting for a Davis Cup final. Irrationally we retain the memory of twenty thousand people lubricating parched throats with cans of beer at White City or Kooyong under a burning Australian sun. Somehow, three hundred freezing spectators huddled under blankets while coyotes yowl at the desert moon doesn't quite fit. But perhaps we have Harry Hopman to blame for that. In the postwar heyday of the Davis Cup he helped turn the competition into an Australian festival.

Provided you were watching from the protective warmth of the Mission Hills Clubhouse, that desert setting with the huge silver moon hanging overhead had a charm all of its own, as Buster Mottram saved the possibility of an embarrassing rout by fighting his way back from the brink of extinction against Brian Gottfried. And, of course, when the sun was up to warm the icy desert air during the afternoon the stands were nearly three quarters full. But the sizeable band of British fans who had journeyed six thousand miles to cheer their heroes had a right to wonder why more of southern California's vast tennis playing population could not stir themselves to drive the odd hundred miles to witness the famous and traditionally exciting event.

Paul Hutchins spoke out vigorously against the long-touted idea of a condensed two-week Davis Cup held among eight or sixteen qualifying nations at one venue along the lines of the World Soccer Cup. But certainly the present tortuous and confusing format needs some urgent revision so that, at the very least, more planning can go into the staging of the final.

The idiocy of the present setup was highlighted by the fact that on the very same weekend America was staging the 1978 final, Mexico was being eliminated by Colombia in an early round of the 1979 competition. How is the poor confused tennis fan supposed to understand that?

But despite these recurring problems, there were some very positive aspects of a contest that was played throughout in a pleasing atmosphere of camaraderie between two teams who respected each other's abilities.

From an American point of view the biggest plus was the continued growth of the remarkable John McEnroe. By crushing John Lloyd in the opening singles and Mottram in the decisive fourth rubber on Sunday for the total loss of only eleven games, McEnroe created a new record for singles play in a Davis Cup final. The previous best was twelve—a round shared by such notables as Bill Tilden and Björn Borg.

It had been evident right from the start that the U.S. needed two singles victories from McEnroe to remove the distant threat of an upset, and that was asking quite a lot from a nineteen-year-old arriving from a grueling indoor European tour—especially since he had never played singles for his country before.

But McEnroe, channeling his Irish temperament into two periods of intense and unwavering concentration, rose to the challenge with performances that surprised even those of us who consider him to be the greatest talent currently wielding a racket.

"Not even Connors or Borg has made me look that much of an idiot," remarked John Lloyd. But at least Lloyd managed to break the McEnroe serve. Mottram, like Borg in Sweden four weeks earlier, never got to deuce.

Against Mark Cox and John Lloyd's brother David in the doubles, Smith and Lutz produced as fine a demonstration of the art as one could have wished for. They first played together when McEnroe was five, and it showed. Their defense was watertight and their offense—especially from Smith at the net—devastating.

When I caught Smith peeking at a video cassette recording of the match at a party given by Mission Hills assistant pro Tommy Tucker on the Saturday night, he grinned and said, "Just checking on our mistakes." . . .

Mottram's feat of fighting back from two sets and match-point down in the third against Gottfried was a triumph for a player whose erratic past performances have frequently defied logic. Despite two agonizingly unlucky net calls on vital points and no less than eleven foot-fault calls, the big Englishman refused to allow anything to distract him from his single-minded determination to dig himself, and Britain, out of a large hole. The fact that he succeeded established him as a competitor of the highest rank.

It took John McEnroe to tarnish Mottram's brilliant 1978 Davis Cup record, but then, as the coming months will prove, McEnroe is something else.

McEnroe has done more than enough to justify that prediction, but my crystal ball was a great deal cloudier when, earlier in the article, I suggested that it would be Britain rather than the United States that would benefit most from the 1978 Davis Cup campaign. Although Paul Hutchins feels that there were spin-off benefits in Britain as a result of his team's success, there is no doubt that more could have been made of it. In contrast, the emergence in that tie of John McEnroe as a Davis Cup player par excellence laid the cornerstone for a nationwide revival of interest in the competition in the United States.

Despite the morale-crushing defeat McEnroe and his colleagues suffered in Argentina in 1980, the 1981 semifinal victory over Australia at Portland, Oregon, and the revenge exacted over the Argentinians in the final in Cincinnati were two of the most enthusiastically supported Davis Cup ties I can remember in the United States over the past fifteen years. Although the old maxim, which insists that the game and the event be bigger than any individual, is both desirable and frequently true, the fact has got to be faced that the prime reason for the widespread interest in America's fortunes in the 1981 Davis Cup was the participation of John McEnroe. With the greatest respect to everyone else involved, the Davis Cup would never have justified the Nippon Electric Company's one-million-dollar worldwide sponsorship had not McEnroe, as the world's No. 1 player at year's end, been on hand to offer his own very special brand of talent and excitement. The reaction of the average American sports fan was typical: "The Davis Cup's gotta be a big deal if McEnroe's playing." Right or wrong, that is the way the peripheral follower of the game thinks, and even though the excitement McEnroe created was not always appreciated by the traditionalists—not even, indeed, by his own captain—two things would almost certainly have happened if he had joined Connors and stayed away. Argentina would have won, and no one would have cared.

But McEnroe has never stayed away, no matter how poor the opposition or how inconveniently a tie might fit into his own schedule. Facing Ivan Lendl on a suffocatingly hot day at Flushing Meadow in the Davis Cup quarterfinal was not the way he would have chosen to celebrate his Wimbledon triumph. But that was what he had to do just five days after surviving the physical and emotional ordeal of beating Borg at the end of a very long fortnight. Small wonder that it proved to be beyond him, but with Connors making a rare appearance on the team, McEnroe recovered in time to deliver the *coup de grâce* against Tomas Smid in a conclusive fourth rubber and so deprive Czechoslovakia of the Cup they had won in Prague only seven months before.

For reasons best known to the man himself, that was the first and last America saw of Connors as a Davis Cup player that year, but with Tanner stepping in to score a vital five-set victory over Peter McNamara in the semifinal against Australia in Portland, Jimmy's absence was shrugged off by a team that had learned to live without him often enough.

Ashe, however, found it more difficult to shrug off the behavior of his doubles pair when McEnroe and Fleming threw a fit over a complete misunderstanding between the umpire and a linesman. As the Americans were beating McNamara and Phil Dent handsomely at the time, the conduct warnings they received as a result of the rumpus that brought Ashe on court in the not-very-effective role of peacemaker seemed all the more unfortunate and unnecessary.

It was, however, an absolutely typical example of the kind of trouble that erupts when McEnroe—and equally in this case Fleming—simply will not tolerate a genuine mistake that an umpire stubbornly refuses to rectify. Fleming had stopped playing because the linesman behind him had called the ball out. The call had been quiet, so that only Fleming and not the umpire heard it. It had also been wrong. The linesman admitted as much to Fleming but refused to tell the umpire, because the rules say that the umpire is supposed to *ask* his line judges before they can offer information of that kind. One is reminded of Mr. Bumble in *Oliver Twist* who would have had the perfect answer to such stupidity. "If the law supposes that," said Mr. Bumble, "the law is a ass."

Quite true, but ranting and raving about it wasn't going to get them anywhere, and they should have let the matter drop after an initial protest. But, of course, they couldn't, and with the dignified Ashe out there trying to placate two overwrought players, the whole scene descended into a distasteful farce. McNamara and Dent couldn't understand it. If ever there was an example of the basic difference in Australian and American attitudes toward sport, this was was it—not that McEnroe and Fleming were the first to illustrate the gulf that separates them. Dennis Ralston and Chuck McKinley had been lambasted in the Australian press back in the early sixties for their behavior in Davis Cup play; and in their reaction to this latest incident, McNamara and Dent voiced opinions that echoed those of Neale Fraser (now the Australian captain) and Roy Emerson twenty years before. "We think it's special playing for Australia," said Dent. "And it must be bad when you get two warnings when you are playing for your country. I reckon it was a pretty poor show."

McNamara was bewildered and obviously disgusted. "I find it hard to believe that they made such a big deal out of nothing. The game's deteriorated somewhat. You're supposed to have thirty seconds between points and we waited around for five minutes. If we had got another set, there is no way we would have lost the match. They would have been defaulted out of it because under Davis Cup rules the third warning means 'exit.'"

But to McEnroe and Fleming the issue of whether they were winning or losing or whether the incident reflected well on themselves or their country was obviously secondary in their minds to the fact that an injustice had occurred, and injustices must not be tolerated.

"Anyone who makes a decision like that shouldn't be allowed on a tennis court," McEnroe told a packed press conference afterward. "We're the ones who pay in the long run; we're the ones who are made to look bad as a result of a decision like that. The question is not whether the ball was in or out. That wasn't the point. The point was that play was interrupted by an erroneous call which the linesman freely admitted and the umpire refused to accept."

"Yes, I'm sure the crowd misunderstood as usual," added Fleming. "I'm sure they thought we were complaining about the call, but we weren't because the ball was in. But, of course, then the din starts up and it just makes everything more tense and difficult."

But McEnroe knew they had overreacted and tried to explain why. "It might sound like bullshit to say something like this, but you get uptight because it's not only you playing out there. That is the difference in playing Davis Cup. You definitely feel worse if you lose. Not that everyone in the whole country is wondering what's about to happen in Portland, Oregon, but there are a lot of people who are still patriotic and care about it, and you try to do your best for them. And I get uptight. I think you could see I was more nervous than normal."

That explanation cut little ice with the Aussies. When Neil Amdur

Before real problems erupted between them in Portland and Cincinnati, McEnroe was more than happy to take Arthur Ashe into his confidence during the Davis Cup ties. *Russ Adams*

of *The New York Times* relayed McEnroe's explanation of nervousness to Dent, the reply was laced with sarcasm. "He never acted like that before? God, he gets nervous a lot, then."

Primarily the Australians were annoyed that they had become the victims of the inevitable but unintentional chain reaction that is set in motion in these situations. The officials were the original offenders, firstly for making a mistake over a line call, which is perfectly understandable, and secondly for refusing to bend stupid rules so as to defuse an incident with a little common sense. The Americans were then at fault for continuing to argue so long because, in doing so, they broke the very legitimate and very necessary thirty-second rule. Four or five minutes is a long time to hang around on court, trying to maintain both concentration and body warmth while your opponents argue over a point of law.

Back at the Marriott Hotel that evening, jubilation at having clinched the tie 3–0 was tinged with feelings of regret in the American camp over the row. It had spotlighted the seemingly unbridgeable gap that existed between Ashe and two of his players—a gap that had more to do with upbringing than difference in age. It had been drummed into Arthur by his father and his tennis mentor, Dr. Johnson, that the No. 1 rule in life for a black trying to make it in the white man's world was never, ever to give anyone the opportunity to reproach you for misbehavior. Consequently Ashe, who is as nervous as a kitten inside, has very rarely let his emotions show. McEnroe and Fleming, of course, were never placed in that position. For them the need to fight for what was right was one of the first principles of life. But, even if he agreed, Ashe just felt they went about it the wrong way.

"I thought their behavior was disgraceful and I told them so," Arthur told me when I ran into him in the corridor outside McEnroe's suite. Inside John and Peter were each on their third beer. But even though they were high on victory, they had not lost sight of the fact that the needless row had created problems within the team as far as their captain was concerned.

"We blew it," McEnroe said, suddenly and momentarily morose as he let the facts sink in. "I know, don't tell me, man, we blew it."

In a sense they blew it again against Argentina in Cincinnati three months later. But it was indicative of the enormity of the triumph they achieved that McEnroe should leap into the arms of his captain Arthur Ashe and trainer Bill Norris after he had brought the Cup back to America by beating Jose-Luis Clerc in the decisive fourth rubber. He had barely spoken to Ashe for the previous forty-eight hours. Once again two hopelessly different temperaments had been trying to work for a common cause and had found the task well-nigh impossible.

Ashe was simply too low key for McEnroe—and, it must be said, for other members of the team as well—and McEnroe, in turn, was operating at a pitch of emotional endeavor that Ashe could barely understand. In the end, victory was the only possible palliative.

This McEnroe provided, more than ably abetted by Fleming in the doubles, with as brilliant a display of skill and tenacity under pressure as anything he had achieved before. Considering what was at stake, I think the fifth set he produced against Clerc was probably as fine a set of tennis as he has ever played in his life. After beating Tanner on the opening day, Clerc had proved he could compete at the Americans' own level on the medium-fast Supreme court at the Riverside Coliseum—a court that was supposed to give the United States almost as much advantage as the Argentinians had enjoyed on their own clay in Buenos Aires. And he continued to prove it by leveling his match with McEnroe at two sets all.

McEnroe, however, had not been assisted by what occurred in the American locker room during the ten-minute break between the third and fourth sets. "It was like Fifth Avenue in there," declared Tony Palafox, who had popped in to see if John needed a little tactical advice (Ashe was not saying a word to him on court) and then left quickly when he saw the crowd swarming around the player. "I just told him to keep serving to the forehand and into the body, and then got out of there. I always used to insist on a closed locker room at the break when I was playing for Mexico, and John should have done the same."

Ironically McEnroe had not done so for fear of causing another rumpus. "I just didn't want to make any waves," he told me. "I didn't want to get accused of being any more difficult. I thought we'd had enough problems, but I suppose that was one thing I should have insisted on. Half the USTA seemed to be in there, and so many people were trying to say the right things that I just lost my concentration."

It was not until the fifth set that McEnroe got himself together again and channeled all that ferocious energy and skill into one final, awesome bid for victory.

Despite the fact that the score would only be 2–2 if he lost, McEnroe knew that Guillermo Vilas was well capable of beating Tanner, and his pride would not let him contemplate putting Roscoe under that kind of pressure. In his mind this was the set; this was the match; this was the whole Davis Cup campaign right here, and he was prepared to fight all out for it. There was no more time to yell at linesmen or worry about Ashe. Everything he had learned as a tennis player and competitor was leveled at a strong and worthy opponent, and in the end one felt a little sorry for Clerc. No one would have survived the tidal wave of talent that engulfed him. It was all there: the viciously accurate serving, the masterful change of pace, the flashing winners that seemed to explode out of nowhere past Clerc's outstretched racket, and those mesmerizing drop volleys that wafted off his racket with such spellbinding delicacy.

But it was not just the skill and the shotmaking. John McEnroe was as hyped up as I had ever seen him and yet so obviously in total control. It was intimidating to watch from courtside, so heaven knows what it was like from the other side of the net. "Yea!" he yelled, punching air to celebrate the unloading of another ace. The crowd roared. Father, like so many spectators, was waving a little American flag in glee. Even Ashe leaped out of his chair to applaud.

"My, is this man pumped up!" exclaimed former ATP president Cliff Drysdale in his role as TV commentator. "This is a truly remarkable performance."

And indeed it was. The eventual score in that fifth set was 6–3, and Clerc did well to get three games.

The celebrations were long and noisy. Back at the hotel, rock music blared in McEnroe's suite as well-wishers, some welcome and some not, poured in. "The walls," wrote John Edwards graphically in the *Daily Mirror*, "thumped like an elephant's heart."

It wasn't all Edwards had to say. As a newcomer to the tennis scene, but a veteran and much-lauded observer of everything from Vietnam to the Royal Wedding, Edwards had obviously been shocked by the vitriol that poured out of McEnroe in moments of high stress. Edwards was not alone in this. ITF president Philippe Chatrier, a former French Davis Cup captain, was appalled at some of the things McEnroe said to USTA officials sitting at courtside.

The worst of it had occurred on the second day in the doubles, which, no matter how much one disapproved of the antagonism that broke out on court among the players, became compelling entertainment. At one stage Ashe had to order McEnroe back to the baseline as he and Clerc advanced toward each other like gunfighters in Dodge City. But the best drama lay purely in the tennis. The score of 6–3, 4–6, 6–4, 4–6, 11–9, with Vilas serving for the match at 7–6 in the fifth (there are no tie-breakers in Davis Cup), was extraordinary enough in itself, considering that Clerc and Vilas were two unfriendly singles players trying to weld themselves into a doubles team born of necessity rather than desire. But the level of skill displayed made it as fine a game of doubles as I have ever seen, for all four men played at the top of their form, not least Fleming, who was something of a revelation. He was on court with three of the best six singles players in the world, yet no one would have detected that he was, in that sense, the odd man out from the way he held steady when the heat was on, serving brilliantly and volleying with savage power.

Guillermo Vilas, seen here with the racket he helped design before switching to the Slazenger mid-size prototype. Armed with his new British weapon, the Argentinian won Grand Prix titles in Rotterdam, Milan and Monte Carlo in the spring of 1982. *Slazenger*

But throughout that great victory and the first four sets of his match with Clerc, McEnroe apparently felt the need to continually carp and frequently abuse the officials. Once he called a middle-aged black linesman "boy," which was about as stupid a thing as he has ever said in his life, not merely because it was unpardonable but because, as he has proved over and over again, he has no racial prejudices whatsoever. But there is no doubt that his prejudices against everyone who sits in authority over him on a tennis court are very real and very alarming. There have been wrongs on both sides, but it is vital that the venom be kept in check if the deep-seated distrust he feels for officials is not to seriously impair his brilliant career.

15

A CHARITY AFFAIR AND
A TV COMMERCIAL
FOR BIG BUCKS

The rain was slanting across the 59th Street Bridge on one of those nights that turn New York into the wettest, windiest and most impossible city in the world. The Checker cab, finally secured after half an hour's splashing down Second Avenue, was crawling over the East River toward Queens at a speed that seemed to reflect the driver's reluctance to leave the cabbie's haven of Manhattan behind.

"Look, see the lighted bubble?" said the passenger pointing through the partition down toward his right. "That must be it."

But it wasn't. That much became obvious some minutes later when no more than a few members' cars stood in front of an establishment that, on investigation, turned out to be the East River Club—a tennis club, to be sure, but not the right one.

Trying to console himself by the sight of his meter ticking up dollars in the darkness, the driver backed out and headed on down Vernon Boulevard, the cab dwarfed by the forbidding blackness of the large, deserted buildings. It is no-man's-land down there in the shadow of the bridge, a seemingly unpeopled buffer of warehouses and storage lots lying between the sprawling dormitory of Queens and the concrete forest of Manhattan. It is the sort of place where the Mob dumps its bodies. You expect to see George Raft, his collar turned up against the rain and his hat dripping, emerge from the shadows, light a cigarette and step into a big, black limousine. It is not a place for those frightened of the dark.

Like its neighboring club a few blocks away, Tennisport, which was located eventually by the sight of Cadillacs and other big, black limousines causing a minor traffic jam down on Second Street, has recently given a reason to visit to the kind of people who would prefer to pretend the area didn't exist. Tennisport has a plenitude of courts, a comfortable lounge, restaurant and bar and a stunning view of Manhattan.

"Something going on here?" asked the driver superfluously.

"Yea, Borg's playing," replied the passenger, who was in no mood to get into the kind of discussion that the mention of other names might elicit.

In fact Björn Borg was far from being the only international celebrity who had trekked through the wastelands to congregate at the oasis of glitter and glamour Tennisport was providing that evening. Like one of his guests, David Frost, Vitas Gerulaitis has a knack of being able to call up celebrities by the limousine load when he needs support. And the Vitas Gerulaitis Youth Foundation, which holds a series of clinics for inner-city kids in the New York area during the summer, needs and gets superstar support.

Some ten thousand youngsters have received free rackets and instruction since Vitas got the program under way in 1978. A couple of the most promising have been sent to Harry Hopman's Tennis Camp in Florida, which has certain advantages over a back wall in the Bronx.

There was no instruction going on this particular evening—just Vitas, Björn, John McEnroe and Peter Fleming attempting to offer $150 worth of entertainment for the kind of crowd who like to be where the action is. "Everyone looks as if they've just arrived from Florida—or spent the whole week under their sunlamps," observed *Tennis Week* editor Linda Pentz as the rain pounded down on the corrugated roof.

The chairman of the Watford Football Club, a British second-division soccer team, recognizable even under a wide-brimmed black hat, seemed to be one of the few who had gone without sun. But Elton John, a longtime tennis buff, who has discovered that tennis tournaments—albeit on a modest scale—come cheaper than buying soccer clubs, now has a place to go and bronze himself every January: the Half Moon Hotel in Antigua, where he is donating prize money for a small pro tournament.

Alan King, one of the ATP's earliest and most faithful supporters, was at the microphone, introducing the players and being amusingly abusive to anyone he set eyes on.

Borg, mindful of whose event it was, carefully managed to lose to Gerulaitis 6–4 in an energetic one-set encounter; and after Fleming had struggled to put up some kind of resistance against McEnroe, John and Vitas played out the final with Harry Hopman in the chair. Even in a serious situation that would be one person guaranteed, I would imagine, to command McEnroe's respect as an umpire, but, of course, under these circumstances the scourge of officialdom was content to parody himself. Twice he feigned anger over some decision, and soon Hop was feeding him lines.

"John! Score, please, I've forgotten it," Hopman called out.

"Forty–love," replied McEnroe, trying to conceal a sly grin under an expression of mock anger.

"Thirty–fifteen," replied Hop deadpan, sidestepping the con.

McEnroe was too exhausted to keep the comedy going for long, and he didn't care about the outcome. He was there because he had told Vitas he would be, but the previous week had been draining emotionally as well as physically, and he wasn't able to derive much real amusement out of the occasion.

"But he always supports us," Peter Fishbach, one of the foundation directors, explained to a visitor in the locker room afterward. "Even this summer when he had been unable to commit in advance because he had been unsure of his schedule, he showed up anyway—just like that. It was a complete surprise and, of course, we were delighted. It's because of the support we receive from John as well as people like Ilie Nastase, Arthur Ashe, Fred Stolle and the guys here tonight that we have been able to raise over $100,000 in four years."

At $150 a ticket, the Tennisport exhibition was helping to pour more dollars into that fund, but the guests were getting more for their money than a low-key exhibition and the see-and-be-seen syndrome. Tables for three hundred people with a huge buffet had been laid out over three adjoining courts, and it was here that the New York tennis set, the insiders and those rich enough to masquerade as insiders, gathered after the matches. But if in a tennis sense Vitas Gerulaitis, by virtue of his personality as much as his proven talent, is Prince of the City, there is no disputing who is King. But as yet John McEnroe had not appeared at the postmatch festivities.

In the meantime there were plenty of famous faces for the voyeurs to ogle. Elton John and David Frost, of course. Philip Martyn, the former world backgammon champion and occasional traveling companion for Vitas on the pro tour, was there casting an approving eye over the three gorgeous girls decked out in Cacharel dresses (one of the evening's sponsors) who weaved their way elegantly between the tables handing out miniature bottles of perfume to women who were already bathed in something similar.

And, of course, there were the real players—Gene Scott, former U.S. Open semifinalist and still one of the world's best exponents of the royal original game Real Tennis or Court Tennis; Carole Graebner, ex-wife of Clark and a women's singles finalist at Forest Hills in 1964; Dick Savitt, Wimbledon champion of 1951, who continued to hit what the pros call a "heavy" ball on courts around New York for many years after that. Henry Bunis, son of that dapper citizen of Cincinnati Al Bunis, who founded the Grand Masters tour and eventually sold it to Mark McCormack for a cool million, was at Savitt's table. Henry's a player, although strictly a part-time one now, having collected what remained of his scattered sanity after a few globe-trotting years on the pro tour and put his talents to better use in the more static—and some would say saner—world of banking.

The wine, courtesy of Martini & Rossi, who seem to be into something other than aperitifs these days, flowed. Vitas swept in, grinned at his scarlet-clad sister Ruta, greeted a fellow whose hairstyle and dress were reminiscent of a British Teddy Boy circa 1950, and then huddled with International Management Group director Bob Kain, whose job in life is to organize the multimillion-dollar careers of Vitas and a certain Mr. Borg.

This then was the New York tennis stage and its players, most of whom had made their entrances long before the future king had picked up a racket. It was still not a world in which the new monarch felt particularly at ease. But it was his world and he was only then just beginning to comprehend just what kind of power he could exercise over it. But not this night. When he did eventually appear, slipping in virtually unnoticed to stand alone by the bar, dressed in white jeans and a maroon silk shirt, he looked like a man more interested in exits than entrances.

Peter Fleming was with Jenny Hudson over on the far side of the huge three-court area, as was Kay McEnroe, alone with some friends since her husband was out of town. John, with that faraway look creeping into his eyes, surveyed the scene. If he hadn't just won the Davis Cup for America two days before, stayed up until 5:00 A.M. celebrating, flown back to New York to see the Rangers play at the Garden, gone to a dinner at Le Club, spent six hours doing a television commercial for Dunlop out on Long Island, and been about to move into his new duplex apartment on East End Avenue the next day, he might just have been able to whip up a little enthusiasm for the party. But the man was exhausted, and no wonder.

The television commercial had been enough to test anyone's endurance, let alone someone coming off a pressure cooker of a week at the end of a long season. And, of course, for McEnroe in particular, it tested his patience. As any actor will tell you, the glamour in filmmaking lies strictly in what appears on celluloid. Putting it there is often a tedious and repetitive performance, and McEnroe's temperament is not well suited to tedium.

But he arrived at the designated location punctually at 10:00 A.M. and was still there—complaining a bit by that time, but still there—at 4:30 P.M. Locating the place had been the least of his worries, for the commercial was being filmed at the Cove Racket Club, the place where

EVER NOTICE WHAT RACQUET McENROE PLAYS?

The still-photo version of the television commercial that McEnroe filmed for Dunlop at the Cove Racquet Club. *Dunlop Sports Company, 1982*

he had started his regular training stints with Tony Palafox in 1976. He could have found his way there blindfolded. Not that he had to. In five years he had progressed from a local hopeful with above-average talent to a millionaire who arrived in a chauffeur-driven car, which was probably just as well. Millionaires tend to have million-dollar headaches after two consecutive nights of celebration, and it was a good thing that Palafox, still the tennis director at Cove, was there to break the ice and help with some stand-in shots while John tried to get some coffee inside him. It was something of a testament to his reliability that he was there at all. By the time the crew had got all their bits and pieces together, he was actually ready to get the thing rolling before they were.

Three of the indoor courts had been cleared for the proceedings, which required McEnroe to hit shots fired at him from a ball machine with a racket whose normal handle had been replaced with a transparent staff. The idea behind this rather bizarre piece of remodeling of the "McEnroe Maxply" was to facilitate the eradication of the entire racket in the final film. McEnroe, in fact, would be seen hitting a ball with no racket in his hand at all. A few frames later—abracadabra, hey presto and surprise, surprise, it would be a Dunlop.

That it was a Dunlop and not a Wilson or some other American racket would appear, on the surface, to be something of a coup for the famous British company that has been supplying the Maxply brand to players big and small for longer than most of us can remember. However, that is not quite the case. In a strange story of intercompany poaching, Dunlop stole what was in fact a Slazenger initiative. Many people who see the brand names Dunlop and Slazenger emblazoned on pieces of tennis equipment at virtually every tournament they watch in Britain may be unaware that, although Slazenger jealously guards its own identity, it is in fact owned by Dunlop. So there was some hard-nosed business sense behind a decision that created no little bitterness in certain sections of the conglomerate.

The idea of signing McEnroe to an exclusive racket contract as soon as he was free from his Wilson contract at the end of 1980 was John Barrett's. Although better known as a BBC television commentator and tennis correspondent of the *Financial Times,* Barrett, one of the great activists and enthusiasts of the game in Britain, is actually employed full time by Slazenger as its tennis director. It was he who first approached John McEnroe, Sr., at the Masters in New York in January 1980 and set the ball rolling for the U.S. Open champion to become a Slazenger player after a long and well-received discussion at Mr. McEnroe's law offices on Park Avenue.

Both father and son were adamant that a racket, almost identical with the regular-sized, wood-framed Wilson that John had been using throughout his career, must be specially made and then marketed as a McEnroe model. Barrett agreed, and at only the second attempt the Slazenger craftsmen came up with a model that met with the player's approval. Terms of $300,000 per year over five years were proposed, and during the Benson & Hedges Championships at Wembley later that year, Barrett and his Slazenger boss, Ian Peacock, laid on a presentation that clearly impressed McEnroe. That was hardly surprising because the company had gone to considerable trouble and expense over a new line of equipment. The line included luggage and head covers in extravagantly designed red, white and blue with McEnroe's name all over the place, as well as a new design for the actual racket. The racket was, of course, of prime importance to John, and although some companies in the Far East and Europe did dangle a little more money in front of him, he was quite content to accept a little less for a superior product.

However, when the whole deal was presented to the head man, Alan Lord, who oversees both companies, he felt that if such a huge financial investment was going to be poured into one product it should carry the bigger and better-known name. The fact that Dunlop had a more efficiently organized marketing setup in the United States also carried weight because, obviously, that was where the biggest sales were likely to accrue. Lord gave Peacock a last chance of saving his baby, but the escalating financial demands were rapidly moving out of a viable price range for Slazenger. In the time that had elapsed, McEnroe's worldwide title-winning achievements had precipitated a flood of dollar-laden offers from other companies which quickly outstripped the original offers from Slazenger and Wilson, whose initial attempts to hang on to their star never looked like succeeding. So Dunlop, agreeing to meet all McEnroe's technical demands, shouldered the financial burden which, in effect, guaranteed the player three million dollars over five years. There were some people down at Slazenger headquarters in Croydon who were, to put it mildly, a little miffed.

Nevertheless, despite the obvious disappointment it caused in some quarters, the switch did make sense, and after a few false starts, Dunlop also came up with a racket to suit McEnroe's specifications. McEnroe was grateful that even though his Dunlop contract was signed and sealed and due to begin on January 1, 1981, the company agreed to allow him to play that year's Masters with his old Wilson. Changing rackets can be a traumatic experience for a professional player. After a few years' use—especially those formative years when a player is making his way to the top—his racket becomes part of him, an extension of his arm. Any other racket, even one of similar design, feels like an alien limb that has been grafted on. Even his carefully designed new Dunlop felt strange to McEnroe when he first started using it at the WCT tournaments in Milan and Frankfurt in March 1981, but the fact that he managed to win both titles, beating Björn Borg in the final in Italy and Tomas Smid in Germany, helped enormously to erase the psychological barrier that was waiting to fall the moment there was any hint of loss of form.

In detailed technical terms, the McEnroe Maxply is a completely different racket from the Dunlop Maxply so many of us picked out of the cupboard at home and used to hit a tennis ball for the first time. (Ironically it was a Maxply that McEnroe used the first time he played the game at the Douglaston Club. But he soon made a permanent switch to Wilson.) The original Maxply has a head that is too light and too flexible for McEnroe's style. He wants power and control, and that means a stiffer frame and a more even balance. Even the first models of the new racket were still too light in the head for his liking, so he added ten grams of lead tape down either side to help the balance.

He also wanted a completely different grip. Previously Dunlop rackets had a basically round grip, while McEnroe had become used to playing with the angular shape of grip that Wilson builds. "I reckon it's easier to feel where the racket head is with an angular grip," McEnroe explains. "And as I play a lot of angles and spins, it's important to have a precise feel."

The grip size is 4⅝ and the racket weighs 13½ ounces strung. Even though he uses a much lower tension on his strings than Borg (around 50 to 52 pounds, depending on the machine), he still goes through over a hundred sets of gut a year.

Although the new racket has been designed to McEnroe's personal specifications, the exact same racket is now on sale to the general public. It costs a little more than the old Maxply, which, incidentally, is still used by many pros on the circuit, including the 1982 WCT World Doubles champions at Birmingham, Balazs Taroczy and Heinz Gunthardt.

To their credit Dunlop and Slazenger (who designed a new model for Guillermo Vilas) both saw the need to counter the swing to larger frames and a variety of newfangled materials and acted swiftly. In doing so this British company has gone a long way toward saving the traditional tennis racket from extinction. If it were not for McEnroe and Vilas, as well as Björn Borg with his Donnay and Jose-Luis Clerc with a normal-sized wood Rossignol, the Prince-type large-framed rackets would have virtually seized control of the entire industry. But the fact that four of the top six men players in the world (not forgetting Chris Evert Lloyd with her Lady Wilson) still use instruments that actually look like a tennis racket has maintained a healthy balance.

No matter how much prestige is attached to having the No. 1 player in the world use your product, the ultimate worth of the whole operation lies in the sales growth. Does a racket or a shoe or any piece of sporting equipment sell better because it is endorsed by a star player? The answer is determined to some degree by the quality of the star. In the case of a Jack Nicklaus, a Borg or a Pele it has been proven affirmatively over and over again. But what about a superstar like McEnroe with an image problem? Does unpopularity among significant sections of the public (especially, in this case, parents who may not want their children aping what they perceive to be the bad image McEnroe portrays) have an adverse affect on any potential boost in sales? Not, apparently, in America. In the five months following his victory at Wimbledon with the old Maxply, U.S. sales had rocketed by a barely believable 240 percent.

No one was more surprised than David Branon, vice president of marketing for Dunlop in Greenville, South Carolina. "I had predicted a growth of between 60 and 75 percent based purely on the stores' willingness to order more rackets as a result of the publicity it was getting," Branon told me. "So 240 percent was staggering. It has far exceeded our wildest dreams."

Branon and I were watching Joe Matza, director of the commercial film unit, position McEnroe in front of the camera.

"We want the racket to stop right about here—or right about where it would naturally stop after a topspin forehand or whatever," said Matza, guiding the player's arm through a stroke.

"I don't understand technical details like that," McEnroe deadpanned. "You'd better ask my coach Tony."

Palafox grinned and lined up the ball machine so that McEnroe could swing at the correct angle for the cameras. "He's used to this machine. I used to turn the thing on when I was coaching him and he couldn't get the ball over the net," Palafox joked. "No point in wasting my time, was there?"

His famous pupil smiled and went into another routine of aiming forehands at a white board erected as a target area just to the side of the camera. Technicians ducked as balls started flying through the air. Accuracy was not that easy to achieve under such circumstances, even for the No. 1 player in the world. But as long as he was occupied, McEnroe was happy enough. It was the hanging around between takes that gnawed away at his patience, grating on that side of his nature that has given birth to the reputation that now precedes him everywhere. Matza and his crew looked like men treading through a minefield most of the day and were obviously both surprised and relieved to encounter little more than a few squibs of irritability. But then, when it comes to living up to his commitments, McEnroe is the complete professional, hung-over or not, and there are numerous "star" performers in all spheres of the sporting and entertainment industries who give back a lot less for their dollars than he does.

Dunlop, at any rate, is more than content. While John wandered off to nibble at some ravioli that had been produced for the crew at a makeshift canteen, I continued my discussion with Branon and Robert Weiner, vice president of the New York public relations firm that handles the Dunlop account. Hadn't there, I wondered, been a reluctance to invest so much money on a player with such an obvious image problem?

"Well, the people at the head office in England took a very positive attitude about it all," Branon explained. "They decided they wanted to update the old Maxply image, and to do that properly they needed the very best player available. Obviously that was McEnroe, and despite the bad publicity he received at Wimbledon, he's done the job. Mind you, I think he's far more popular than people realize. After Wimbledon, the letters we received were running about fifty-fifty for and against, and those that were for were really *for* him. His fans are real fans, no doubt about it."

EPILOGUE

John had just returned from an exhibition tour in Europe when we sat down to talk in the lobby of Stouffer's Hotel in Cincinnati. "I feel better about things," McEnroe announced out of the blue. "I feel I've grown up a bit. I don't know why—it's just a feeling."

It had only been nine months before in Milan, when the subject of a book had first been raised, that I had suggested that he ought to wait at least until he had won Wimbledon before consigning his thoughts to paper.

"How about waiting until I grow up first?" he had replied with another little flash of blinding honesty.

There had been a fair amount of growing up taking place in the intervening months, most of it concealed from the public eye beneath that unfortunate façade of rudeness, anger and resulting controversy. But only fools fail to learn from adversity, and McEnroe was learning a great deal about himself and the complex world around him during the long, frustrating winter months of 1981–82. For a young man who had the tennis world at his feet at Flushing Meadow back in September, it was not a particularly successful period, despite the Davis Cup triumph in Cincinnati.

But, in many ways, it was more important for McEnroe to win a few battles with himself than with his opponents on a tennis court at this stage of his career, and by the end of another unsuccessful Volvo Masters in January, there were signs that he was succeeding.

It had taken a few more setbacks, however, before the medicine started to take effect. From a personal point of view, the Benson & Hedges Championships at Wembley proved to be precisely the kind of disaster he had anticipated. After gaining an easy two-set-to-love lead over Connors in the final, McEnroe became so upset by the attitude of the umpire and certain sections of the crowd that, for the first and probably the last time in his life, he found he could not summon up the will to fight. The match was lambasted in the press as a disgrace to

Pause for contemplation before the ultimate confrontation in a stormy Benson & Hedges final at Wembley in November 1981, which Jimmy Connors eventually won in five sets. *Syndication International*

sport, with even the sedate London *Daily Telegraph* carrying pictures of the two players over four columns on its front page. Inevitably McEnroe took the brunt of the criticism because Connors has learned to mask his indiscretions with sly little gestures that could, I suppose, be termed humorous. But no matter what the press had to say about it, a very large number of people present were not fooled.

In fact, the pro-McEnroe mail received by *Tennis World* and *Tennis Today* was staggering not merely for its quantity but for the amazing uniformity of opinion expressed by what were obviously the tennis-educated sections of the crowd.

"It was the biggest mail we've ever received on one subject," said Ron Atkin, the consultant editor of *Tennis World*, "and 98 percent was saying, basically, that McEnroe got a raw deal."

A random selection from those letters will suffice to cover the points made by virtually all of them. For instance, Mrs. L. Leigh, of Carleton near Blackpool, wrote to *Tennis World:*

I am not usually given to writing to magazines, but after watching the Benson & Hedges final I felt so sickened and sad that I just had to put pen to paper. The way the umpire and the crowd treated John McEnroe you would have thought they were dealing with the devil himself. I'm sorry, but all I could see was a young man, scarcely more than a boy really, looking thin and drawn with his nerves jangling like church bells. His tennis is nothing short of brilliant. Surely we should nurture his talent and try to help him with his psychological problems instead of trying to destroy him as we did at Wembley?

Another *Tennis World* reader, J. A. Hughes, of Barrow-on-Humber, wrote:

Why can't the administrators try to understand players more instead of trying to turn them into mindless and emotionless machines? John McEnroe is the first to admit that he does not always behave as he should, but can we not be more tolerant of someone who just happens to be bluntly honest? Let's face it, when he calls an umpire stupid, he is usually right.

Writing to *Tennis Today*, E. S. Williams, of Stafford, said:

I am writing to complain about the disgusting treatment John McEnroe received during and after his match with Connors at Wembley. Although I am a McEnroe fan, I make no excuses for his behaviour and I can understand that he deserved a warning for hitting a ball into the roof. However, I feel that the seemingly biased attitude of the umpire was totally unjustified. Connors went unpunished for offences similar to those of McEnroe, and the umpire did not make a single comment when Connors left the court and joined the public (an offence in itself). . . . Certainly the attitude of officials leaves much to be desired. If he is treated like a recalcitrant five-year-old, it is hardly surprising that he chooses to behave like one. Of course he should know better, but then shouldn't we all?

Miss J. E. Churchill, of Plymouth, was "absolutely disgusted" by the way McEnroe was treated by the Wembley crowd. And also in *Tennis Today*, Miss N. A. Hunt, of Bury St. Edmunds, wrote:

I feel very sad about what has happened to John McEnroe. To see the most brilliant and inspired player the world has ever known reduced by people's unfairness and cruelty to an emotional wreck within the space of a couple of hours, was the most upsetting thing I have ever witnessed in ten years of following tennis. There were some of John's friends in the crowd but we could not heard above the majority who thought it was their duty to batter the young man into the ground. . . . I hope for everyone's sake that this has not permanently damaged his career.

In fact the whole upsetting affair might have helped, in the long run, to have the opposite effect. Although he never expressed it to me in so many words, I think what shocked McEnroe most about the Wembley final was that he allowed the baiting of the crowd and the apparent bias of umpire John Parry to sap his competitive drive. For a man who believes that it is demeaning to give anything less than one hundred percent, that would have troubled him deeply.

It may even subconsciously have helped spark the vehemence of his reaction to Ivan Lendl when they met in an exhibition tournament in Milan a few weeks later. After a couple of bad line calls, Lendl appeared to give up, and the large crowd soon sensed he was merely going through the motions.

"At the changeover halfway through the second set, John started abusing Ivan and calling him all the most terrible names," said the tournament promoter, Sergio Palmieri. "Ivan, of course, got very angry when John accused him of not trying and went out and played very hard and won in the end. So John actually did himself no favor, though from our point of view he saved the match as a spectacle. Yet for everybody else it was Ivan who looked like an angel and John the devil."

The fact that he cost himself an easy victory did not concern McEnroe very much. For him it was a point of honor. A century ago, I fancy, he would have been a very uncompromising man to face with a pistol for a duel at dawn.

His ability to look defeat squarely in the eye and accept it unflinchingly was also much in evidence the next time Lendl beat him. This time the match was for real, and so was the margin of the Czech's victory. In front of eighteen thousand New Yorkers in the semifinal of the Masters at Madison Square Garden, Lendl clobbered his great rival 6–4, 6–2. If anything, the score flattered McEnroe, who never served well enough to stem the floodtide of pounding ground strokes that engulfed him. John had been playing with a strapped thigh all week because of a slightly pulled hamstring, and mentally he was far from sharp after a row with the tournament officials who told him, erroneously, that he had won his group in the round-robin format when in fact other complicated permutations were possible. Irresponsibly McEnroe went off to a midnight rock concert in Greenwich Village the night before a supposedly meaningless match with Teltscher and eventually paid the penalty when he lost to Eliot the next day. It meant that he missed out on the $30,000 bonus awarded to group winners and ended up playing Lendl in the semifinal instead of Gerulaitis.

Inevitably he was asked if either the injury or the row over the rules had affected his play. "If I allowed myself to use those sorts of things as excuses, I would have no right to call myself a professional tennis player," McEnroe told the press fifteen minutes after being humiliated

"To be or not to be: that is the question
Whether 'tis nobler in the mind to suffer
The slings and arrows of outrageous fortune
Or to take arms against a sea of troubles
And by opposing, end them."
                                        —Hamlet

That, indeed, was the question facing John McEnroe in 1982. *Melinda: Phillips Studio, New York* by the man to whom he least enjoys losing. "I played disgracefully, and he never allowed me to find a proper rhythm."

Back in the locker room, trainer Dave Fechtman smiled when he heard about that reply. "He's a tough cookie, that's for sure. I must admit I wasn't too keen on him at first, but like just about everybody else who has gotten to know him really well, I've developed a lot of respect for the guy. John's one hell of a human being."

People one step removed from him, even a few of the other players who think he is a pretty easygoing locker-room companion, find that a little hard to believe. "How can he be that great a guy when he is so rude to people all the time?" one young pro asked me recently. It is a good question and one that McEnroe is just beginning to realize he will have to answer or lay to rest through a change of attitude.

After the defeats in Tokyo, London and New York, John realized that the pressure he was putting on himself by accepting the typecast role of bad guy was starting to affect his play. But was he capable of changing?

"I don't know, but I'm going to have to try," he told me. "I don't want a whole generation of young players behaving like idiots and everyone saying it's my fault. But, believe me, I don't go out there to create a disturbance. I just get so unbelievably frustrated when mistakes are made. Then when I get angry over something that happens, I get angry at myself for being angry. After that I just get this feeling that I've blown it again, so what the hell?"

In fact there were definite signs of improvement in the weeks following the Masters debacle. He won the U.S. Pro Indoors in Philadelphia, generally regarded as the world's most prestigious indoor title, by dismissing Connors with surprising ease in the final. Almost the only time he blew up at a linesman during the whole week was to intervene on a call that had gone against his semifinal opponent, Sandy Mayer.

Having been beaten by the talented Californian Trey Waltke in the first round the year before, McEnroe had much to prove in Memphis two weeks later, but although he made it to the final he was unexpectedly denied the title by the new Australian Open champion, Johan Kriek.

Again the week had passed mainly without incident, and there were also better vibes between him and Arthur Ashe when he played against India in the opening matches of the 1982 Davis Cup campaign at La Costa, California.

"You see, I'm trying," he said when he turned up in Brussels in March for what was to have been a four-week European tour. "It will take people about a year before they notice any difference, but I've got to start somewhere."

Unfortunately he never had the chance to prove his point that month, for just before his quarterfinal match against Israel's Shlomo Glickstein, he trod on some spare rackets lying by the side of the practice court when he chased a wide volley from Peter Fleming, and sprained his ankle. "He was in so much pain afterward I thought he might have chipped a bone," admitted trainer Bill Norris. "But x-rays revealed no more than a pretty bad sprain."

After Norris had strapped McEnroe's ankle, Grand Prix supervisor Ken Farrar came into the locker room to confirm that McEnroe was having to default. The first time Farrar put the question, he received no answer. With time ebbing away he was forced to press the point, and a look of pain crossed McEnroe's face that, this time, had nothing to do with any discomfort he was suffering from the ankle. "Oh, yes, I suppose so," he snapped. Then he hobbled toward the door and, turning to Peter and me, muttered. "God, it burns me up having to admit that—just saying it hurts. And at the quarterfinal stage, too!"

He was just as frustrated when I phoned him a couple of weeks later at his new apartment on New York's East Side. The ankle had turned all kinds of nasty colors by the time he had arrived home, and the WCT event in Strasbourg, which Lendl eventually won at a canter, and the Grand Prix tournaments in Milan and Frankfurt had all been crossed off his schedule.

McEnroe seemed to be heeding the advice of his doctors and consoling himself with practice on his electric guitar as he waited for the injury to heal. He knew that a premature return could wreck the chance of meeting the challenges awaiting him in the summer, and with Ivan Lendl now throwing a giant shadow over his shoulder, it was vital that he should be renewed in both body and mind.

Neither was he in mint condition when he arrived in Dallas for the WCT Finals, more than five weeks after the accident in Brussels. He had eased himself back into action with two exhibitions against Vijay Amritraj and Roscoe Tanner before flying off to Tokyo to play the four-man Suntory Exhibition. He lost first to Vilas and then to Van Patten in the third-place play-off. Björn Borg eventually won the event but within seventy-two hours was losing to Dick Stockton trying to qualify for the Alan King Classic in Las Vegas.

Suddenly a combination of tennis politics and injury had left the two men who had dominated the game for the previous two years looking like pale shadows of their former selves. Although a major question mark hung over Borg's future, McEnroe's problems appeared simpler to overcome. Still voraciously hungry for success, John just wanted to get himself fully fit and match-tight.

"I need to play," he told me on arrival in Dallas. "I'm pretty insecure about my game right now because I am not moving well and the ankle swells up even after a few hours on a plane. I just hope I get my confidence back quickly."

Bill Scanlon nearly buried that possibility right at the start of McEnroe's attempt to defend his WCT title. Given the circumstances, Scanlon was one of the last players John would have wanted to come up against as he tried to ease himself back into competitive play, and when he faced the first of four match points in the fourth-set tie-break, it seemed that the Texan, loudly supported by his hometown crowd, was on the brink of another startling victory.

Until then, McEnroe had been revealing all the insecurities that afflict an athlete who is worried about his fitness and form. As usual, he was not finding it easy to deal with Scanlon's incisive volleying and flat-hit strokes that stayed low on the medium-paced Supreme carpet at the Reunion Arena. But overcoming technical problems is one thing, restoring confidence quite another. And all the hesitation of a player lacking match practice was evident as McEnroe missed no less than fourteen break points on Scanlon's serve during the course of the match.

Considering the opportunities lost, it was hardly surprising that John found himself staring down the barrel of a gun as Scanlon maneuvered himself skillfully through the early part of the fourth-set tiebreak. But for a champion of McEnroe's caliber, match points trigger a different set of alarm bells to breakpoints. When faced with the ultimate test, steel fibers slot back into place automatically somewhere deep in the champion's psyche. But not so deep as to be a subconscious act. McEnroe knew what he had to do.

"When the match points arrived, I knew it was no good being tentative anymore," he told me later. "I remember deciding to go for it."

Which he did. At 6 points to 4, with one Scanlon serve to come, McEnroe saved the first match point with a topspun cross-court pass off the backhand and the second with a heavy first serve down the middle that Bill couldn't handle. Then the old fuzziness returned as McEnroe dumped a bad volley into the net to give Scanlon a third match point.

This time McEnroe floated a pinpoint forehand down the line. Seven-all. But Scanlon came back at him again and reached match point No. 4 at 8–7. Again McEnroe ignored his preferred serve, wide to the backhand in the ad court, and instead ripped a big first serve straight down the middle. Two points later, the pressure suddenly on the other foot, McEnroe clinched it by 10 points to 8 as Scanlon erred.

The eleven thousand crowd rose to both men after that, realizing they had witnessed something special, and as the match entered its fourth hour, Lamar Hunt and his new executive director, Owen Williams, tried hard—and quite successfully—not to look relieved at the passing of a crisis. It was not that they didn't want the hometown boy to win, but rather that a Scanlon victory would have deprived the tournament of the showdown everyone wanted to see—McEnroe vs. Lendl. But Hunt and Williams can both wear the poker face as well as anyone, and it soon became apparent that the match had swung irrevocably McEnroe's way, even though Scanlon battled bravely to regain a lost advantage. The battle was still intense and many games still as closely fought as they had been throughout—a factor that helped make this the longest match in the twelve-year history of the Dallas finals. When McEnroe finally wrapped it up 6–3 in the fifth, it had lasted four hours and forty minutes—about thirty-five minutes longer than the classic Borg-Laver confrontation in 1975.

While Lendl was steamrolling his way past Wojtek Fibak (who actually played well enough to embarrass his young friend for a while) and Vijay Amritraj, McEnroe ensured WCT would get the final it deserved by outlasting a tenacious Eddie Dibbs over three long sets in the semifinal.

The very fact of reaching the final constituted something of a triumph for McEnroe, who had been spending long hours in the treatment room at Reunion Arena every day in an attempt to ease his ankle through the strains of continuous match play. He was under no illusions as to just what kind of a test awaited him in the final, but much of his usual buoyancy had returned by the time he followed Ivan to the podium to address the charity dinner audience at the Hyatt Regency Hotel on Sunday night.

As usual his off-the-cuff speech lacked nothing in directness, but there was more evidence of the charm that is so rarely given a chance to surface in public as he conscientiously remembered to thank various people who had helped make the week in Dallas a success. "And especially Norma, who has been her usual wonderful self," he added.

The remark was both timely and accurate, for Norma Hunt had, once again, sailed effortlessly through another week of unceasing social activity, apparently enjoying total recall when greeting by name reporters, players, officials and all Lamar's wide variety of business associates. But, of all the compliments she received, I suspect nothing touched her more than the charmingly phrased remark from a young man who does not exactly throw his compliments around like confetti.

The final, played for the first time on Monday night, was every bit as tough as McEnroe had anticipated. Lendl, riding a tidal wave of supreme confidence after a seven-month streak that had seen him win 77 out of 79 competitive matches, blitzed his way through the first set 6–2, dropping only one point on his own serve.

The fact that McEnroe managed to stem that tide and all but turn it around was a tribute to his own extraordinary skill and application. If his physical condition was still less than perfect, the New Yorker was certainly in a far sharper mental state than he had been when facing Lendl in the semifinal of the Volvo Masters four months before. He realized that only a supreme effort on his part would prevent the Czech from stealing his title, and in the second set he produced it. Raising the percentage of good first serves to well over 60 percent, McEnroe started exerting pressure with his own delivery while concentrating on blunting the power of Ivan's pounding ground strokes as baseline rallies developed. With his malleable wrist and exquisite timing, McEnroe managed to defuse strokes that would have flattened many other players. For a while Lendl started to lose his rhythm, both off the ground and on his serve, and one break was enough to give McEnroe the set 6–3.

At 3–3 in the third, the fate of the championship was effectively decided. Still clinging to his hard-won and slender advantage, McEnroe reached breakpoint on Ivan's serve. Playing what appeared to be a perfect point, John took Lendl's second serve early and came in. The return floated high and invitingly to McEnroe's backhand. Nine times out of ten, Lendl would have already been on his way to meet the down-the-line volley. Trying to anticipate this, McEnroe hit his shot cross-court, only to find that Lendl hadn't moved an inch. Nor, as it turned out, did he have to, for the volley landed right in front of him—right where, in McEnroe's estimation, he should not have been—and all he had to do was push a forehand back over the net well out of reach.

The defending champion could have picked just about any other spot on the court for that volley and won the point, secured the break and served for 5–3. Given the delicate balance of the match at that stage, it could have been enough to tip the momentum the New Yorker's way. As usual between two players of this caliber, one or two critical points decide the outcome, and when McEnroe later lost his own serve, the magnitude of that miscalculation became apparent.

"Lendl was anticipating better than I was throughout the match," McEnroe admitted afterward, putting his finger on one of the basic reasons for the Czech's recovery, as Lendl steamed on, suddenly looking awesomely confident once again, to sew up a resounding 6–2, 3–6, 6–3, 6–3 triumph that earned him $150,000.

McEnroe had certainly not lost through lack of effort. Although the score could have been closer for a huge sixteen thousand crowd that was thirsting for excitement in true Texas style, the match was packed with incidents. McEnroe found various things to complain about, but in keeping with his attempts to create a better image, he never lost his temper during numerous arguments with a strict but sensibly low-key umpire from San Diego, Ron Bennett.

If the heavily strapped ankle gave him any problems, it never showed, as he flung himself about the court with audacity and courage. Once he hurtled right out of the court in pursuit of a Lendl pass and hit himself in the face with his racket as he fell over a flowerpot and collapsed into the blue curtain draped below the corner boxes. Lendl, who otherwise refused to react to anything that happened on McEnroe's side of the net, walked over to his adversary to ask if he was all right. Later, however, Lendl did not even bother to glance around after a full-blooded forehand, driven from close range, caught McEnroe smack in the chest and knocked him backward.

"I've never been hit that hard before," John admitted as he sipped a beer in his room with some friends later that night. "I didn't realize he was going to go for it until it was too late."

Whether a fourth consecutive defeat at the hands of his rampant rival would bruise his confidence as heavily as that ball had bruised his chest remained to be seen. He was still far from happy about the state of his game and his ankle as he worked his way through the early rounds of the WCT Tournament of Champions at Forest Hills ten days later. He knew his No. 1 ranking was in jeopardy and the challenges of the summer were beginning to look daunting indeed.

At the very least one could hope that the press, the public and the officials would give him time and space to prove that he has the willpower to curb his temper and put a permanent guard around that Celtic fire. That he has behaved appallingly at times in the past is not in dispute, but in an emotional if not a pecuniary sense, he has been made to pay dearly for his sins by people who are all too ready to climb on the great bandwagon of morality in an age that is awash with behavior far more vulgar, senseless and dangerous than anything perpetrated by the subject of our story. Many of my tennis-writing colleagues have realized this, but it took a British television critic, Hebert Kretzmer of the London *Daily Mail,* to put things in perspective when he wrote: "McEnroe seems to be little different from any Sunday golfer who has ever smacked his putter into the ground in a fit of temper. Of course he should know better but shouldn't we all. From the stick McEnroe has been getting, you'd have thought he had mugged a defenceless old lady or burnt the Union Jack in Trafalgar Square. As Thomas Macaulay was once moved to observe, 'We know no spectacle so ridiculous as the British public in one of its periodical fits of morality.' "

New Yorkers, too, would do well to mark those words. However, while McEnroe is a product of New York, he is also a product of the game he plays with unique brilliance, and if the tennis establishment doesn't like the way he behaves, then one can only say its members have been pretty inept in their attempts to do anything about it.

As I write, John McEnroe, for all his volatility and problems with physical fitness, appears to be one of the more reliable and consistent factors in a sport that seems intent on tearing itself apart. In Dallas, McEnroe, who has the intellectual capacity to develop into one of the game's more sensible statesmen, was preaching the lesson of conciliation. "I think it would be better for the game if the two sides got together and worked out some sort of a compromise," he said, referring to the increasingly antagonistic war that had broken out between the Pro Council (as guardians of the Grand Prix tour) and World Championship Tennis. "We need consolidation so that there are more tournaments when all the top players have a chance to play against each other. That is what the public wants to see and that is what is best for the game. But at the moment the top six guys end up in the same event only two or three times a year."

Ironically, that is precisely what the administrators have been trying to achieve with such marked lack of success over the past several years. McEnroe, in his usual incisive style, has seen right through to the core of the problem. But how to solve it, among the collection of battered and sensitive egos involved, is another matter.

For the moment, McEnroe should not concern himself with it too much. He can best serve his sport by continuing to do what he has been doing for the past five years—playing brilliant tennis for his country in Davis Cup and in a whole variety of tournaments all over the world with unflagging dedication and determination, channeling that rage for perfection into the endless pursuit of a champion's noble goal— victory, justly earned. Despite all the growing pains, the excitement he engenders will remain even as the temper fades. And the future is full of promise.

McENROE'S CAREER RECORD

GRAND SLAM SINGLES TITLES
Wimbledon
  1981 beat Björn Borg. 4–6, 7–6, 7–6, 6–4
U.S. Open
  1979 beat Vitas Gerulaitis. 7–5, 6–4, 6–3
  1980 beat Björn Borg. 7–6. 6–1, 6–7, 5–7, 6–4
  1981 beat Björn Borg. 4–6, 6–2, 6–4, 6–3

MAJOR PLAY-OFF TITLES
Masters
  1979 beat Arthur Ashe. 6–7, 6–3, 7–5

WCT Dallas Finals
  1979 beat Björn Borg, 7–5, 4–6, 6–2, 7–6
  1981 beat Johan Kriek, 6–1, 6–2, 6–4

VOLVO GRAND PRIX SUPER SERIES TITLES
TransAmerica Open, San Francisco
  1978 beat Dick Stockton
  1979 beat Peter Fleming

Stockholm Open
  1978 beat Tim Gullikson
  1979 beat Gene Mayer
Benson & Hedges Championships, Wembley
  1978 beat Tim Gullikson
  1979 beat Harold Solomon
  1980 beat Gene Mayer
New Orleans*
  1979 beat Roscoe Tanner
Milan*
  1979 beat John Alexander
  1980 beat Vijay Amritraj
  1981 beat Björn Borg
Richmond, Virginia*
  1980 beat Roscoe Tanner
U.S. National Indoors, Memphis
  1980 beat Jimmy Connors
Custom Credit Australian Indoors, Sydney
  1980 beat Vitas Gerulaitis
  1981 beat Roscoe Tanner
Trevira Cup, Frankfurt*
  1981 beat Tomas Smid
ATP Championships, Cincinnati
  1981 beat Chris Lewis
U.S. Pro Indoors, Philadelphia
  1982 beat Jimmy Connors

* Before the circuits split in 1982, these were combined WCT–Grand Prix events.

MAJOR DOUBLES TITLES
WITH PETER FLEMING

Wimbledon

   1979 beat Brian Gottfried and Raul Ramirez

   1981 beat Stan Smith and Bob Lutz

U.S. Open

   1979 beat Stan Smith and Bob Lutz

   1981 beat Peter McNamara and Heinz Gunthardt (default)

Masters

   1978 beat Stan Smith and Bob Lutz

   1979 beat Tom Okker and Wojtek Fibak

   1980 beat Peter McNamara and Paul McNamee

   1981 beat Kevin Curren and Steve Denton

WCT World Doubles, London

   1979 beat Ilie Nastase and Sherwood Stewart

Note: Up to the spring of 1982 McEnroe had lost in the first round of only three tournaments since appearing as an unheralded qualifier in the Wimbledon semifinals of 1977. They were Wimbledon 1978, losing to Erik Van Dillen; Atlanta 1980, to John Austin; and Memphis 1981, to Trey Waltke.

Index